W9-AEY-349

Value Driven Management

How to Create and Maximize Value Over Time for Organizational Success

Randolph A. Pohlman and
Gareth S. Gardiner

With Ellen M. Heffes

AMACOM

American Management Association

New York • Atlanta • Boston • Chicago • Kansas City • San Francisco • Washington, D. C.
Brussels • Mexico City • Tokyo • Toronto

Special discounts on bulk quantities of AMACOM books are available to corporations, professional associations, and other organizations. For details, contact Special Sales Department, AMACOM, a division of American Management Association, 1601 Broadway, New York, NY 10019.
Tel.: 212-903-8316   Fax: 212-903-8083
Web site: www.amanet.org

This publication is designed to provide accurate and authoritative information in regard to the subject matter covered. It is sold with the understanding that the publisher is not engaged in rendering legal, accounting, or other professional service. If legal advice or other expert assistance is required, the services of a competent professional person should be sought.

Library of Congress Cataloging-in-Publication Data

Pohlman, Randolph.
    Value driven management: how to create and maximize value over time for organizational success / Randolph A. Pohlman and Gareth S. Gardiner; with Ellen M. Heffes.
        p.   cm.
    Includes Index.
    ISBN 0-8144-0485-5
        1. Industrial management.   2. Value analysis (Cost control).   3. Value.
    I. Gardiner, Gareth.   II. Title.
    HD31.P559   2000
    658.15'52—dc21   00-021498

© 2000 Pohlman, Inc.
All rights reserved.
Printed in the United States of America.

This publication may not be reproduced,
stored in a retrieval system,
or transmitted in whole or in part,
in any form or by any means, electronic,
mechanical, photocopying, recording, or otherwise,
without the prior written permission of AMACOM,
a division of American Management Association,
1601 Broadway, New York, NY 10019.

Printing number

10   9   8   7   6   5   4   3   2   1

Contents

Contents

Preface

The nervous CEO of a publicly held electronics firm slashes his organization's research and development budget by 30 percent, against the advice of his executive team, because this quarter's profits have dropped 25 percent and the Wall Street analysts are openly criticizing his performance. Five years later, his firm suffers serious losses when aggressive competitors flood the market with new and improved products.

The worried head of a major division at a large publishing firm avoids taking action against a junior executive who she suspects has been filing false expense-account reports, because she is afraid that such a discovery will make her department look bad, and cost her a major promotion that she has been counting on. Three years later, amidst a flurry of very bad publicity, the junior executive is convicted of embezzling $50 million from the publishing house.

The anxious vice president for operations of a large oil company refuses to approve an expanded maintenance budget for his firm's network of pipelines because his annual bonus depends on holding costs down, and one year later a major pipeline rupture causes millions of gallons of crude oil to escape into a pristine alpine lake. Ten years of ruinous litigation follow.

These examples of bad business judgment, leading to destruction of value for the organizations involved, are all hypothetical, of course, but they have their roots in a very real phenomenon: the belief that the only purpose of a company is to be profitable *now* and that the only value that matters in a firm's existence is the maximization of shareholder wealth *now*. This belief, which many business analysts in this country have subscribed to, has placed tremendous pressure on executives, managers, and employees in thousands of companies to make short-term decisions that often damage their organizations in the long run. Such decisions are often unilateral, almost always poorly thought through, and in some cases fatal. The purpose of this book is to develop and explain a philosophy of management, Value Driven Management, that we believe will help organizations create and maximize value over time if it is practiced faithfully and conscientiously over time. Value Driven Management views profitability and the improvement of shareholder value as one of the results of properly using eight value drivers in the leadership and management of an organization.

In their best-selling 1994 book, *Built to Last,* James Collins and Jerry Porras debunked the myth that visionary, highly successful companies such as Disney and Wal-Mart exist first and foremost to maximize profits. The reality, they note, is quite the opposite.

> Contrary to business school doctrine, "maximizing shareholder wealth" or "profit maximization" has not been the dominant driving force or primary objective through the history of the visionary companies. Visionary companies pursue a cluster of objectives, of which making money is only one—and not necessarily the primary one. Yes, they seek profits, but they're equally guided by a core ideology—core values and sense of purpose beyond just making money. Yet, paradoxically, the visionary companies make more money than the more purely profit-driven comparison companies [companies compared by the authors to visionary companies].[1]

From the point of view of Value Driven Management, the success of so-called visionary companies is no accident: These are firms that consistently take multiple values into account when they make decisions, plan strategy, or develop new products. They are successful precisely because they are value driven, and not solely concerned with seeking short-term profits.

In the pages that follow, we will argue again and again that organizations that balance value drivers in a complex juggling act when they make decisions—and that consistently use these value drivers in their information processing—will outperform firms that do not. Performance, however, is not *just* short-term profitability; although we freely acknowledge that, in market-based economies, firms must be profitable over time, or they will fail. The matter of *how* firms make money is important, naturally, and we deal with this issue again and again in this volume. Common sense tells us that there is more to life than just making money, and Value Driven Management is rooted in good judgment and common sense. We hope that you will find Value Driven Management to be a powerful means of creating value in your personal and organizational lives, as it has been in ours, and that you will find it to be a philosophy of management good for a lifetime—and for a new millennium.

—Randy Pohlman
Gary Gardiner
Fort Lauderdale, Florida

Endnote

1. James C. Collins and Jerry I. Porras, *Built to Last: Successful Habits of Visionary Companies* (New York: HarperBusiness, 1994), 8.

Acknowledgments

First and foremost among the many capable persons who have helped us so greatly in the preparation of the manuscript, we must acknowledge the contributions of our editor at AMACOM Books, Adrienne Hickey and her staff. Their conscientious, careful, and competent editing has made this book a better product in every way. Linda-Rae Hoge, Executive Assistant to the Dean of the Wayne Huizenga Graduate School of Business and Entrepreneurship, Nova Southeastern University, is also owed a special vote of thanks for the many hours she spent inputting sections of the manuscript, for her careful proofreading, and for her creativity in designing the graphics. Barbara Ireland, Administrative Assistant in the Huizenga School, also added her creativity in designing the tables.

Two of our graduate students have also helped greatly. Rimal Slaoui, Research Assistant, has willingly and ably spent hours of her time on the Internet, on the phone, and in the library in successful pursuit of key references and important permissions. Eric Steinberg made a timely and appropriate suggestion for the inclusion of an important and illuminating case study at the very moment we needed such a suggestion most. Kim Penner, Position Manager/Southern Region, Koch Industries, gave us very helpful comments for the manuscript's improvement.

We thank the many faculty members at Nova Southeastern University who gave us their support, encouragement, and constructive criticism to make this a better book. Randy thanks James S. Ang, Florida State University; Barry Baysinger and Bill Beedles, University of Kansas; Ali Fatemi, DePaul University,

Charles Koch, Koch Industries; Eugene Laughlin and Verlyn Richards, Kansas State University; and Richard Roll, UCLA for influencing his thinking throughout his academic career.

Finally, and perhaps most importantly, we must thank our spouses, families, and friends for their continuing support as we labored weekdays, evenings, and weekends to finish the book.

Part I

Value Creation and Maximization Over Time: Value Driven Management as a Comprehensive Philosophy of Management

Chapter 1

Value Creation: There Is No Going Back!

The business environment has changed drastically and dramatically over the past century, and now contains challenges that could not even be dreamed of a hundred years ago. Management theories and practices that have evolved during the twentieth century have all too often been simplistic, unidimensional, and nonintegrated approaches to sophisticated, multidimensional, and complex problems. Value Driven Management is a comprehensive, multifaceted philosophy of management that can change all that.

If there is one thing you probably do not need, it is yet another management book that discusses the tumultuous changes that continue to take place in the business and work environment. Change now defines the *status quo*. Reminiscent of the legendary words of the Greek philosopher Heraclitus, who advised centuries ago that we can never step into the same river twice, in the new millennium, the river is simply flowing faster. We have little choice but to plunge in. What we need is a process for navigating our way through this torrent of continuous and constant change while maintaining our balance and sanity. We must learn to swim in the river, and there is no going back.

The survival process is a philosophy of management—*Value Driven Management*—that is designed precisely to cope effectively with this accelerating pace of change. Value Driven Management begins with a simple premise that we call *The Value Theory: What people value drives their actions*. Whether a business organization adopts Business Process Reengineering (BPR) or Total Quality Management (TQM), or buys the latest and greatest silver bullet offered by a business guru or high-priced consulting firm, each decision made and each action taken involves people—people who work in the organization and in all the other organizations it interacts with. People and organizations (which are made up of people, not simply boxes and lines that appear on organizational charts) value various things. Knowing what an organization values, therefore, and what truly drives its decisions and actions, will help us understand its decision-making processes and how and why it takes the actions it does.

It is almost impossible to read a business newspaper or a newsmagazine or view a television program without reading or hearing a report on the newest big decision of some major organization. Whether it is Apple Computer firing its latest and hapless new CEO, a sudden move by a Fortune 500 company, an employee downsizing of nearly one-third of its American workforce by Levi Strauss, or a multibillion-dollar stock split, value-driven questions immediately come to mind. What was *really* behind the decision? We have become highly skeptical of public relations statements and the spin circulated by some companies. What *really* led to the action the company took? What results are hoped for by taking this action? And what will the actual results be?

Underlying each event are two important and interrelated issues that affect organizations and individuals: What impact will the firm's decision and its subsequent action have on value creation for the organizations involved? And what impact will the decision and subsequent action have on all of the individuals involved, including executives, managers, employees, members of the organization, and its other constituents?

In many ways there is no longer a way we can avoid dealing with such value-laden issues and questions. In the fast-paced, complex, and multidimensional world of contemporary business, decision makers at every level and in every organization simply have to focus on creating value for the firm they work for.

A second major premise of Value Driven Management (VDM) is that for businesses to survive and succeed in the new world, decision makers must create value over time (VOT) for their organizations. If they are unable to create VOT, their organizations will be replaced in market-driven economies by businesses that do. As individuals working in organizations, we need to understand this fact of life in order to achieve our own objectives. As individuals, we are not going to do as well as we can or flourish personally unless we are in organizations with which we are in synch and in which we can contribute value. In this brave and bold new world, success has become a matter of the values of organizations and individuals being compatible and congruent.

Value Driven Management poses several important questions for all of us as individuals. Do we struggle to accept the way decisions are made in our organization? Do we often think that decisions take too long to make and yet are also too short-term oriented? Do we think we would be more effective professionally and personally if we had a philosophical framework to help us understand the decision-making process of our organization (and every organization), as well as understand the powerful and simultaneous impact of eight important value drivers on organizations? We believe that Value Driven Management provides such a framework.

The Need for an Integrated Approach to Management

The experiences of the past have clearly shown that there is a better road for organizations to travel through the twenty-first century. As humans engaged in the production of goods and services, we have struggled with the question of how best to lead and manage virtually since the invention of organizations. While the world has changed dramatically over the last 100 years, the theories and models of management that have evolved over the same period have been conceived or implemented as unidimensional or nonintegrated approaches, and have not changed at the same rapid pace as have the structures of organizations themselves.

Over the past two decades alone, thousands of American firms have laid off more than six million employees[1] throughout the United States, and more than 30 percent of the Fortune 500 firms no longer exist in the form that they were originally developed. Some firms have declined to the point of ceasing to exist as we once knew them, while others have experienced dramatic turnarounds—such as IBM and Harley-Davidson. Many firms that did not exist two or three decades ago have grown to become multimillion-dollar organizations, such as 800-Flowers; and some companies have even become multibillion-dollar organizations, such as Wal-Mart, Dell Computer, Cisco Systems, and software giant Microsoft.

This book is about leading, managing, and working in organizations that are charging into, and through, the twenty-first century, and creating value as they do so. Leading, managing, and working in these successful organizations have roots in traditional theories and styles, but these are styles that will soon become extinct. Primarily because of the fiercely competitive global environment and the powers of technology, the traditional model of organizations, as we know it, is fast becoming as extinct as the dinosaur.

Leading with Vision to Integrate the Parts Is Like Connecting the Right Dots

Components of the new, value-driven organization already exist in scattered parts and pieces. What is needed is a blueprint that integrates the parts. An appropriate analogy is the well-known ''connect the dots'' game. When we view an empty page filled with unconnected dots, we cannot see or know what is really there. The page is a confusing maze of unconnected dots. When we begin to connect the dots, the picture gradually emerges, begins to make sense, and then suddenly springs into focus. The seemingly unrelated dots have been integrated into a meaningful and sensible whole, and the whole is greater than the sum of its parts. The end result is that psychological or perceptual value has been created.

So it is with the organizational dynamics and components that are necessary in order to succeed and prosper in the business environment of today and tomorrow. The capabilities and competencies required already exist; yet, as with the dots, the challenge is to correctly connect the organizational pieces so that every player involved has a clear vision of how value is created.

The real value, then, of Value Driven Management is that it provides a fundamental intellectual and philosophical foundation of how to think about organizations, how to operate in an organization, and how to see yourself as a leader, decision maker, and value creator in an organizational environment. The purpose of Value Driven Management is not to replace other sensible, proven, and effective management practices, but to provide a framework that makes it clear for every person who must make decisions in organizations to see, understand, and deliver the most fundamental result of all: value creation.

The goal here is to put all the pieces together in a comprehensive model: to connect the dots. In working with the value-driven model, we find again and again that successful organizations are those with a vision. They are adept at understanding and integrating the eight major drivers of value: (1) External cultural values, (2) Organizational cultural values, (3) Individual employee values, (4) Customer values, (5) Supplier values, (6) Third-party values, (7) Owner values, and (8) Competitor values. This is a topic to which we will return, and frequently.

The New Value Equation: Integrating Employees and Organizations

Clearly, it is no longer possible to employ a single-minded approach to management and leadership. One of the keys to satisfactorily and successfully working with, as well as in, the new world of organization is to first gain an understanding of two sides of the new *value equation*. This new value equation incorporates the new roles and responsibilities of organizations and people and what each can do, jointly and individually, to create value.

The terms *value* and *value creation* will be discussed and described often throughout these pages, and from many different perspectives. An underlying message here is that we often view organizations as beings and even give them human qualities. In reality, any business organization is simply a legal entity; whether it is organized as a sole proprietorship, a partnership, or a corpo-

ration, *people* run it. Organizations do take on special characteristics and in some ways seem to have a life of their own, but they
are always made up of people—people who drive the organization and its culture. The culture of the organization is created by
individuals who come together to form groups in the process of
producing goods and services. An organization's culture, then, is
what its members choose to make it. The organization itself does
not have values; it is comprised of people who bring their values
to their work. These personal values join with and become part
of the organizational culture. For example, an organization itself
cannot be greedy or evil or altruistic. Only the people it employs
can do or be such things, and as a group can create an organization that responds in ways that may be depicted as greedy or evil
or altruistic.

What people value causes organizations to have cultures and
acquire the reputations they have. World-class companies usually
have cutting-edge technology, superior management systems,
outstanding electronic systems, and database management, but
their reputations all come back to human beings—the people
who make decisions and take actions in these organizations,
while using technological and management systems and tools.
One of the critical characteristics of successful companies is a
careful balance between the values, interests, goals, and objectives of the organization, and the values of the individuals who
work for it. The globalized workplace and a new generation of
employees are driving these differences: a value equation is
emerging that is truly unique.

New Means New, and Not Just a New Package!

The savvy new millennium consumer is not easily fooled. Three
generations of marketeers have taught us all a lesson: The package may be new and improved, but all too often it is the same old
soap in a glitzy new box. In the late 1950s and early 1960s the
American auto industry, which has been notoriously slow to
achieve enlightenment, introduced a concept called "planned obsolescence." To pump up sales of new cars, the big three manufacturers—Ford, Dodge, and Chevrolet—would introduce "new"

models of the entire major makes every year. Alas, the new models were not really new; they had just been given a face-lift. The exterior of the vehicles—sheet metal, chrome, and the like—was changed annually, while the guts of the cars—engines, transmissions, and drive trains—remained substantially the same. The savvy American consumer was not fooled. The "new" cars were often plagued with production and mechanical defects, partly as the result of the constant changes in design. At that same time a whole new wave of well-made foreign imports—Volvo, Volkswagen, and Toyota—was hitting the marketplace. Planned obsolescence rapidly succumbed to unplanned obsolescence, and suffered an early death. American consumers were beginning to value true quality in their automobiles, and the value-creation revolution was upon us.[2]

The new business world demands genuinely new products, new solutions, new methodologies, new skills, and new processes. Face-lifts, silver bullets, and quick fixes will not get the job done, although consumers the world over, particularly in America, have always been suckers for any snake oil salesman. Along with these new and real operational necessities, a whole new business mindset, accompanied by a new vocabulary, is emerging.

According to James Lowe, a senior editor at Merriam-Webster, 20,000 words have been added to the unabridged edition of *Webster's Third New International Dictionary* published in 1998 —words that have achieved credibility and staying power, after their initial entrance into the English language.[3] Most of these new additions are words that were nonexistent when the last major new edition of the 450,000-entry dictionary was published in 1961. Not surprisingly, many of the new entries are business terms. In addition to scanning a new print-version dictionary, one need only access a computer system's spell check function to learn the approximate age of the software. Words that have become synonymous with change in business and organizational life, like *re-engineer* and *benchmark*, and acronyms such as TQM (Total Quality Management) and BPR (Business Process Reengineering), were not standards five short years ago. Even the spell check function itself (and the term that describes it) is new!

The new breed of organization is also spawning a new breed

of worker: the knowledge worker. A 1994 article in *Business Week* magazine by Peter Engardio entitled "Have Skills, Will Travel—Homeward," describes the evolving portability of information-based job skills.[4] In this new environment, job security comes not from the promise of a cradle-to-grave employment contract, but from the acquisition and constant upgrading of skills. This new group of workers consists of individuals oriented more toward personal success, than to organizational success alone; where their first loyalty is to themselves and their own careers rather than to their employers. As Gary Gardiner points out in an earlier book, *21st Century Manager*, a new opportunity has emerged to create value: the concept of a fair exchange of services between consenting adults who engage in a mutually beneficial contractual relationship, rather than the employer acting as a parent in a parent-child relationship.[5] This emerging new reality of the workplace and workforce creates opportunities and challenges for employers and employees.

By the year 2025, three-quarters of the workforce in this country are expected to be employed in knowledge-based or service-related positions. As the shift to a knowledge-based workforce continues, quality-of-work-life and quality-of-life issues will obviously become more important to employees and employers.

The cover story feature in *Fortune* magazine in August 1994 reported on high-powered executives who had hit major career turning points and began to "heed voices from within."[6] In many cases a restructuring or downsizing caused the loss of a prestigious and all-encompassing job. In one example, an executive who had suffered a serious heart attack began considering less stressful and life-threatening career options. The article also described how many major companies have initiated programs to help individuals reflect on their careers and lives.

Today's educated and skilled workers do not have to have heart attacks or be victims of downsizing to begin reassessing their career choices. In a high-employment technology-rich economy, knowledge is power. In today's environment, intellectual capital is gaining credibility as a highly prized organizational asset, giving more people more career options than ever before. When an individual is just embarking on a career, or has reached a career midpoint—or even when a person has made substantial progress in the proverbial climb to the top—it may be time for that person to decide what their individual value drivers are and what constitutes a balanced life. Too often, however, individuals are not equipped with the right intellectual and philosophical tools to make optimal career and life decisions, and therefore create value over time for themselves. The Value Driven Management process provides a framework for thinking through and resolving such important problems, and for deciding such things as whether you are in the right part of your organization, the right organization, or the field that is right for you. The exercises that appear at the end of this chapter illustrate the power of the value-driven approach in making major career decisions.

In a society that constantly demands new and better products and services, almost anyone can be fooled by the hype and hoopla that surrounds the introduction of new and improved business approaches and processes, often by high-powered consulting firms or management gurus. Many of these ideas turn out to be short-lived fads, but even some of the best and brightest business professionals then are fooled by the next "new and revolutionary" theory, whether this be Management by Objectives (the rage in the 1960s, but now as dead as a doornail), or Theory Z (hot as a pistol in the 1980s, when Japan was believed to be the world economic superpower, but now just another historical relic), or Total Quality Management (a sensible approach to management that many firms and managers viewed as a surefire silver bullet, yet often poorly implemented). Skepticism and cynicism are two understandable outcomes of the American love affair with organizational silver bullets, and it would not be too surprising if our experienced and knowledgeable readers simply dismiss Value Driven Management as yet another quick fix. Make no mistake, however, Value Driven Management is a philosophy good for a lifetime, and for any age. It is also a philosophy that must be carefully absorbed, deeply understood, and practiced faithfully throughout a lifetime.

Beware of the Danger of Using Outdated "File Folders"

As each of us makes this passage through life, we make sense of all our experiences by organizing them in a collection of "file folders" in our minds. Psychologists call this process concept formation, and it is a uniquely human ability.[7] It is an ability that makes us smart, by allowing us to sort and categorize information from our experiences, but it can also get in our way when we encounter new and unfamiliar experiences. The mental filing systems that we all have are of great value since they help us cope with our personal and business worlds. We keep track of and remember things, are able to describe things using a terminology that is familiar, and deal with routine problems (such as traffic lights) without much conscious thought.

These filing systems become normal and natural habits of mind, or mindsets, allowing us to get through life without having to rethink every situation that we encounter. We all use hundreds of them every day of our waking lives. In a way, they are our mental quick fixes because we use them automatically and quickly in about 99 percent of the situations that we normally encounter, and thus they are of real psychological and mental value for us. The four-dots exercise on page 18 neatly illustrates the problem they can create for us. However, when we encounter a situation requiring a new file folder, we can fail (sometimes dramatically) to solve the problem because we cling rigidly to an old folder.

The familiar picture reproduced in Figure 1-1 also illustrates the tendency to use established mindsets to deal with new problems. Even if we have seen the so-called *old woman/young woman* picture before, we frequently struggle to see both images, even when we know they are there. The first file folder we use to put the picture in—young woman or old—is the one that we tend to go on using. If our established folder is "old woman," the required new folder—"young woman"—may be very hard for us to create. How many of you *still* cannot see both images, even if you know they are there? Our creative MBA students have added to the difficulty of it all in recent years by telling us that they sometimes see an American eagle or a hungry vulture in the picture.

The tendency that we all have to hang onto old mindsets or file folders in new situations produces a number of problems in life for us: a real fear of, and resistance to, change; a tendency to believe that we are always right, and everyone else is wrong; a view to see the changing and complex new world as a threatening

Figure 1-1   The old woman/young woman picture.

place; a tendency to overreact in stressful situations; and a significant reduction in our creativity, and open-mindedness.[8] In
cases of extreme rigidity, there is strong unwillingness to recognize change. We yearn for a past to which we can never return.
When our file folders are outdated, we will often file new information in old folders, even when the new information does not
suit the folders.

When Randy Pohlman was head of Human Resources at one
of America's largest privately held firms, Koch Industries in Wichita, Kansas, and in the course of doing consulting work at major
corporations, he saw numerous cases of people who had worked
in their fields for a long period of time thinking they had seen it
all. For these people, genuinely new ideas were dismissed or re-
jected as old ones whose time had passed. Empowerment, for
example, tended to be written off as nothing more than a new
version of participative management. The reason, of course, is

that they saw these new ideas as old ones that fit into an existing file folder. In most cases, too much experience in the same field led to a serious inability to accurately perceive new developments—a phenomenon we have come to call the file-folder effect. Dr. Ovid Lewis, former president of Nova Southeastern University, also had an appropriate label for such behavior: "hardening of the categories."

When our file folders have become seriously outdated and we have not learned to create new ones, we can rapidly become dysfunctional in a world in which change is real and ongoing, and in which we are regularly required to cope with new problems, new technologies, new ways of working, new employee/employer expectations, and a host of related changes in the new world of business. Closed-mindedness and inflexibility have a predictable outcome in this world: early—and forced—retirement! More than ever before, those of us who do not want to fall victim to workforce layoffs and downsizing need skills and attitudes that allow us to continue to grow, to add skills through a lifetime of training, and to cope with the accelerating pace of change.

A New Way of Looking at Value Creation and the "Bottom Line"

Bottom line is an expression that has become a cliché in our society. The term generally mean *getting results*. For businesses that operate in a free-market economy, "making the bottom line" means profitability, but often with a very short-term emphasis or orientation. Businesspeople tell us that they need to make the bottom line today or they will be out of business tomorrow, and the CEOs of major publicly-held companies assure us that they had better make their bottom line every fiscal quarter or they will soon be out of a job!

In contexts other than business, the term *bottom line* may be more than a cliché and have a certain cachet. "Bottom line, it's the finest restaurant in town." We are gourmets, and our gut reactions (pun intended) are to be respected. "Bottom line, it was a great movie." Now we are distinguished movie critics.

Issues of social and cultural elitism aside, however, the term can be misleading in a discussion of what constitutes *real* value creation in owning, operating, or managing a business. When bottom line is used to mean profitability (as it most often is), it focuses on only one aspect of creating value for the business, albeit a very important one. Businesses that are not profitable eventually go under, of course, or at the very least endure repeated lawsuits from unhappy stockholders and great internal organizational turmoil. Yet when we focus on profitability as the sole means of creating organizational value, we are reverting to a unidimensional way of thinking that is far too simplistic in the complex new global business arena.

We tend to use the same type of unidimensional thinking in individual courses in the MBA and undergraduate programs in business. In operations management courses, efficient scheduling and just-in-time deliveries may become the bottom-line issues. In marketing courses, where the customer is always king and market share is queen, doing almost anything to please the customer and increase market share is the bottom line. Finance classes teach us that the shareholder is king, and so on. In most business degree programs, in recognition of this fact, a final capstone course entitled "Business Policy" or "Strategic Management" is offered in an attempt to integrate individual courses and pull the entire program together.

Value Driven Management looks at the bottom-line issue from a new perspective: The organization's bottom line is creating value (including profitability, of course) from a complex blend and conscious integration of eight value drivers, including external cultural values, organizational cultural values, individual employee values, customer values, supplier values, third-party values, owner values, and competitor values.

A vital component of this process is the new value equation, integrating organizations and individuals. When individuals work in organizations with which they are in synch—ones in which they can use and develop their skills, grow and learn, make contributions, and look forward to going to work—they not only will create value for themselves as human beings, but they will usually also create value for their organizations. Creating business programs at the undergraduate and graduate level that blend this philosophy into every course offered may be our most powerful tool for implementing the value-driven concept in the organizations of tomorrow.

Value Creation, Twenty-First Century Style: There Is No Going Back!

We have now entered an era when the amount of knowledge doubles itself every five years or less, when the number of users of the Internet increases at the same or an even faster rate, and when the pace of change continues to accelerate at an alarming—or exciting—rate. It is a time when people and organizations have no time to waste. The focus of business in the new millennium will be on results, but results looked at from a new perspective: results that create value, the end product of enlightened multidimensional decisions and actions. While achieving positive results is always the goal of successful organizations, so too is the avoidance of disastrous, unintended, and unexpected results. The conscious, conscientious, and systematic use of the principles of Value Driven Management provides a promising tool kit for achieving results in the challenging future that is already upon us.

Exercise 1-1

Creating Value by Making a Proactive Educational/Career Choice

You are the manager of a production department at the XYZ Manufacturing Company in a southeastern city. You are forty-two years old, have been with the company twenty years (ever since you graduated from Great State University with a bachelor's degree in economics), and have been a department manager for the last twelve years. Your company has downsized twice in the last five years, and you feel lucky to still have your job. Because middle management ranks have been hit hard by the layoffs, you see no prospect whatsoever of a promotion; indeed, you are still a bit nervous about keeping your present job for a year or two more, because rumors keep sweeping through your company that there will be still more downsizings.

After talking things over with your spouse, you decide to enroll in Nontraditional Adult University's MBA program for adult learners, which is offered in a convenient weekend format in your city. You realize that the MBA program will be a significant commitment for you because the classes meet every second weekend (with the exception of holiday weekends) for an eighteen-month period. The program coordinator has assured you that you will not be the oldest student in the class, since your age is about average for adult learners in the program.

Since your company is paying for about 80 percent of the tuition and fees, and since you already have strong computer skills, you decide to enroll in the program. The university requires that you take two prerequisite courses, both of which you can do online, before you begin taking the regular MBA classes.

Questions for Discussion and Reflection

1. If managerial decision-making or problem-solving styles were classified on a continuum from *proactive* (forward-looking and strategic) through *reactive* (failing to anticipate problems and then having to react to them) to *overreactive* (reacting to problems with hysteria and authoritarian behavior), which of the three styles best describes your decision to invest eighteen months of your life in a weekend MBA program for adults? Do you see some elements of all three decision-making styles in your choice?

2. Will your decision to complete an MBA program add value to your life, or will it reduce or destroy value? If you think it will add value, can you easily *quantify* the amount of value that will be added, or is it in most ways subjective?

3. We usually think of our personal values as *positive*. What positive values influenced your decision to enroll in Nontraditional Adult University's weekend MBA program: (a) increased income and career opportunities, (b) better quality of work life, (c) increased job skills, (d) improved marketability, (e) new friendship and socialization opportunities, or (f) some other positive values? What clashes did you experience between these values, and other positive personal values, like quality leisure and family time? In making your decision to enroll, how did you reconcile or balance the conflicts or clashes that you may have experienced among your values? Was there a single factor critical in making your decision?

4. What negative factors or motives may have influenced your decision to enroll in the MBA program?

5. Although you discussed your decision with your spouse, and a number of your friends and colleagues at work, who was responsible for making the choice, even if turns out to be less than successful?

Exercise 1-2

Learning to Use New File Folders and Break out of Old Mindsets: The Four-Dots Puzzle

Look at the pattern of four dots reproduced on this page and connect all four of the dots, using no more than three straight lines that must not cross each other. You may not use curved lines to connect the dots, and there must be no open sides remaining in the figure you draw to connect the dots. You can do the puzzle right here in the book, or draw your own dots on a separate piece of paper if you wish.

•   •

•   •

When you think you have the correct answer or if you give up, turn to Appendix A at the back of this book and look at the correct answer. Then answer the discussion questions that appear on the next page.

Questions for Discussion and Reflection

1. What prevented you from solving the four-dot puzzle immediately, even if you have seen it before? What partial solutions did you attempt; perhaps a Z or a U to connect the dots?

2. You have undoubtedly heard the cliché: "You've got to learn to think out of the box." When you first attempted the four-dot puzzle, had you boxed yourself in?

3. What led to the creation of your new file folder for the puzzle, if you in fact solved it? Did you begin to reject failed alternatives? Did you experience a creative breakthrough, an "Aha!" moment, when you suddenly saw the answer?

4. Did you notice other individuals solve the puzzle if you did it in a classroom situation? How did you feel about that? Did you compare yourself (in terms of intelligence) with the other people attempting to solve the puzzle?

5. What emotions did you experience as you attempted to solve the puzzle? If you felt frustrated and angry, did that help you break out of the mindset that you had to stay within the boundaries of the square or rectangle that you saw? Did you create psychological or mental value for yourself when you finally solved the puzzle?

6. Did you learn any lessons from the puzzle that might help you in future problem-solving situations?

Case 1-1

Leadership Does *Matter: Fast Eddie Crutchfield of First Union Bank*

In an era in which critics and commentators complain about a long-term decline in leadership in virtually every aspect of American life—government, industry, and the academic world—it is particularly refreshing to discover that dynamic leaders are very much alive and living in the United States and achieving great things, even while sometimes making serious mistakes. "Fast" Eddie Crutchfield, chairman and CEO of Charlotte-based First Union Corporation is a case in point. In his 36-year career at the bank, he has strung together a series of acquisitions—making more than 80 deals in 12 years—that have made his company the sixth-largest bank in the United States, with assets of over $230 billion in 1999.[9] He earned the nickname, "Fast Eddie," precisely because of the rapid string of deals that led to the bank's phenomenal growth—almost all of them acquisitions of banks located on the East Coast of the United States.

While his exterior persona is that of a folksy "good old boy," he is in fact a hard-driving executive with a reputation for pushing his subordinates hard.[10] Writing in *US Banker*, John Milligan notes that "... ever since he joined First Union out of business school in 1965, Crutchfield has driven himself as if he was still playing football for the Albermarle (NC) Bulldogs. As a banker, Crutchfield has been spurred on by his belief that financial services will soon be dominated by a small number of giant companies—and he intends to make certain that First Union is one of them."[11] By the end of 1997, his total compensation package totaled more than $19.5 million, and he had become a favorite of the Wall Street analysts, largely because First Union's stock price had increased by over

150 percent since 1995 as it successfully absorbed a string of other banks.

Through 1998, First Union had performed well compared to other large banks, but it was its initiatives in other areas that had most impressed Wall Street. Crutchfield has aggressively developed a sales-driven culture at First Union, changing the bank's compensation system so that virtually all branch personnel work on an incentive system based almost entirely on sales increases, and has developed new channels for reaching customers such as Internet banking, a series of minibranches, and a huge new centralized call center in Charlotte. To support such ventures, one of banking's largest data warehouses was built, which gave it the operational flexibility to develop customized sales pitches to individual customers.

The so-called Future Bank concept, which Crutchfield and First Union began implementing well ahead of other banks, was most fascinating to the analysts, however. Crutchfield scheduled a systemwide rollout of the Future Bank by the end of 1998, and its implementation attracted a good deal of publicity. In a nutshell, the Future Bank is ``. . .a push to move scores of routine functions out of branches so employees have more time to sell bank products.''[12] The bank's branches were reconfigured so that greeters would meet customers coming in, and divert them away from tellers and lending officers (whose services cost the bank well over a dollar a transaction) and toward automated teller machines—or ATMs—which can handle transactions for about 25 cents apiece—and to telephones located in the branch that allowed customers to contact the call center in Charlotte. The Future Bank would presumably support a sales-driven culture and bring about improved customer service and satisfaction, allowing First Union to enter the new millennium with record earnings.

Alas, whenever we (and the learned analysts of Wall Street) heap praise upon a company, it seems to immediately encounter difficulties, and this is exactly what happened at First Union. Earnings, and the stock price, plummeted in 1999. Part of the difficulty was the expensive acquisition (far too expensive, the analysts now say) by Crutchfield of Philadelphia-based CoreStates Financial Corp. in 1998 for $17 billion. The company was forced to cut costs, and in March 1999 it fired 5,800 workers. The layoffs alienated many customers who resented the loss of ``face time'' with tellers and other bank employees, and what they saw as an attempt to shuffle them off to phone kiosks and away from people. First Union was forced to hire 2,000 new tellers in an attempt to win back the customers it had lost. ``This is in response to customer requests,'' said First Union spokeswoman Virginia Stone Mackin. ``We underestimated the customer's need for 'face time.' ''[13] Fast Eddie's most recent acquisition and the customer alienation that resulted had put First Union in a difficult situation, although the bank was hardly a basket case. Its earnings dropped to ``only'' $873 million in the second quarter of 1999, and its market capitalization of about $45 billion made it a very expensive acquisition target for a rival such as Wells Fargo, Chase Manhattan, or Bank One Corporation.

As First Union entered the new millennium, its stock was still in the doldrums, and there was continuing speculation that it would become a takeover target. Writing in *The Washington Post*, Kathleen Day noted that its disappointing earnings ``. . . have diminished Wall Street's confidence in the company and caused the bank's board to shake up management in July (of 1999).''[14] One of the casualties of executive restructuring was John Georgius, Crutchfield's longtime second in command, whose retirement was announced. Many commentators expressed the view at the time that Georgius—who was instrumental in the 1980s in developing the unified computer system that facilitated First Union's growth by allowing it to absorb acquired banks quickly and efficiently—was taking the fall for the bank's financial problems. In an article entitled ``Business: Managing for Growth,'' *The Economist* commented, rather critically, that Eddie Crutchfield has declared that he will not attempt any more takeovers, at least in the short run, because First Union is still struggling to absorb what it has already bought.[15]

Despite Fast Eddie's and First Union's present difficulties, do not be too quick to count the bank out. When A. G. Edwards Analyst David Stumpf described Crutchfield as a true visionary,[16] he was expressing a view that is still widely shared by intelligent observers of management. Stay tuned, as the saying goes, for further developments in the case, and for continuing changes in the banking and financial services industry.

Questions for Discussion and Reflection

1. Would you describe Eddie Crutchfield as a proactive, reactive, or overreactive CEO?

2. What strategic moves has he made during his career as CEO of First Union that have created value for the bank? Which value drivers does he seem to have weighted heavily in his decision-making process?

3. Does rapid growth automatically create value for an organization like First Union?

4. Is Fast Eddie Crutchfield a visionary in the way that Ted Turner, for example, is sometimes described as a visionary?

Endnotes

1. Gareth S. Gardiner, *21st Century Manager* (Princeton, NJ: Peterson's/Pacesetter Books, 1996), 6.

2. James Champy, "Mark Twain, Business Consultant," *Forbes*, 11 August 1997.
3. Personal communication to Randy Pohlman from Ellen M. Heffes, 15 January 1998.
4. Peter Engardio, "Have Skills, Will Travel—Homeward," *Business Week*, 18 November 1994, 164–165.
5. Gardiner, *21st Century Manager*, 88–91.
6. Stratford Sherman, "Leaders Learn to Heed the Voice Within," *Fortune*, 22 August 1994, 92–100.
7. Jerome S. Bruner, *Beyond the Information Given: Studies in the Psychology of Knowing* (New York: Norton, 1973).
8. Gardiner, *21st Century Manager*, 48–49.
9. "First Union: Getting the Blues Up North," *Euromoney*, November 1999.
10. John W. Milligan, "What Makes Fast Eddy Run? Part I," *US Banker*, September 1996.
11. Ibid., 39.
12. Rick Brooks, "First Union Officials Meet with Analysts for Long-Anticipated Talks on Strategy," *Wall Street Journal*, 5 August 1999, A10.
13. Kathleen Day, "First Union to Reverse Staff Cuts," *The Washington Post*, 16 December 1999, E1.
14. Ibid., E1.
15. "Business: Managing for Growth," *The Economist*, 31 July 1999.
16. Charles Keenan, "First Union's Chief Seen Unlikely to Go the Way of Bank One's McCoy," *American Banker*, 22 December 1999.

Chapter 2

Values and Value Creation in the Proactive New Organization

> The most important dynamic in the entire world of business and management is what people value. What people value is what drives their behavior. What people value drives their actions, and is a major determinant of the strategy of every business organization. What people value drives free markets the whole world over. Ironically, what people value is also a major cause of problems in organizations!

Albert J. Dunlap and the Sunbeam Corporation: A Case Study in the Short-Term Creation of Shareholder Value

Albert J. Dunlap, former CEO and Chairman of the Sunbeam Corporation, has had a spectacular organizational career, although as of this writing he is unemployed. In his 1997 best-selling book, *Mean Business*, the man the press called "Chainsaw Al" candidly chronicled how he carried out so-called slash-and-burn downsizing tactics at the Scott Paper Corporation, American Can, Sterling Pulp and Paper, and several other companies he had previously been with.[1]

Riding on his previous successes, Dunlap arrived at Sunbeam in July 1996, six months after completing the sale of Scott Paper. The gurus of Wall Street cheered his appointment, according to John Byrne of *Business Week*.[2] Sunbeam's stock jumped nearly 50 percent the day after his appointment as CEO, and within four months Dunlap did at Sunbeam what he had done before: he shut down or sold two-thirds of the company's plants and eliminated half the employees. The stock price continued to shoot upward, but this phenomenon created a cruel paradox for the new CEO. His initial strategy had been to sell the company immediately after slashing through it chainsaw style, but the huge increase in the stock price made Sunbeam unsaleable.

> Although he hired investment banker Morgan Stanley Dean Witter & Co. to seek a buyer last October [1997], no one would pay that large a premium (the stock had risen by 284 percent since July 1996, to over 48). That forced Dunlap to consider another alternative: to scour the market for companies to buy. In early March, Dunlap bought not one, but three companies in one fell swoop: Coleman, the camping gear maker; First Alert smoke alarms; and Signature Brands, the maker of Mr. Coffee.[3]

The seeds of Sunbeam's massive fall in value had already been sown, although this was not apparent to industry analysts at the time. Paine Webber Inc. analyst Andrew Shore, an expert on the household products and cosmetics industries who had been following Sunbeam, was one of the first Wall Street gurus to pick up on some highly irregular practices after Sunbeam announced record earnings throughout 1997. Shore's analysis of Sunbeam's numbers revealed that they had been building abnormally high inventory levels and accounts receivable, that they were "stuffing the pipeline," and that they were giving highly favorable terms to dealers ". . . to ship products aggressively."[4] Shore noticed a couple of bizarre phenomena, the first being a large increase in sales of electric blankets during the third quarter of 1997, when most of these sales normally occur during the winter (fourth quarter). Second, in the fourth quarter of 1997, there was a huge increase in the sale of grills, another seasonal item normally sold in the spring and summer.

Sunbeam had been executing so-called bill and hold deals

with retailers. Sunbeam products were sold at a deep discount and placed in third-party warehouses for later delivery, but the sales were booked immediately. These highly questionable practices led directly to the company's reported increase in earnings, but the game had begun to unravel. The record earnings reported for 1997 ($119 million) were replaced by an unnerving $44.6 million loss for the first quarter of 1998, and analysts frantically began downgrading the stock, discounting Dunlap's claims that he could turn things around. When he was fired by Sunbeam's outside directors on June 13, 1998, cheers were heard around the country, not only from fired former employees, but also from the estranged members of Dunlap's own family. Sunbeam's stock price slid sharply to a level lower than it had been when Dunlap took over.

Dunlap had suddenly become a pariah in a society that had previously lionized him for his dramatic downsizing tactics. David M. Friedson, CEO of Sunbeam competitor Windmere-Durable Holdings, Inc., was quoted in *Business Week*: "He is the logical extreme of an executive who has no values, no honor, no loyalty, and no ethics. And yet he was held up as a corporate god in our culture. It greatly bothered me."[5] Several other executives chimed in with similar comments, but we disagree with them in one key respect. Dunlap clearly valued stockholder value or wealth, and his sometimes ruthless maneuvers had a common purpose: salvaging what was left of a failing company by pumping up the stock value in the short run so it could be profitably sold.

It is not our purpose to demonize Dunlap in these pages, but his behavior illustrates an important point: Executives can have dramatically successful careers, in the short term, by maximizing shareholder wealth. In the process of maximizing stockholder wealth, at least in the short term, Dunlap was paying homage to a widely held belief in the 1990s that investors are the only relevant constituents in a public corporation. A surprising number of otherwise intelligent, astute, and sophisticated financial analysts adopted this unidimensional point of view in the last decade, but it is a view that we will question time and again in these pages.

Dunlap's own words are often beguiling. In a 1997 interview with Ellen M. Heffes, when he was still riding high at Sunbeam, he repeated the major tenets of the management beliefs that he also describes in detail in *Mean Business*:

> I happen to believe business is simple. I think anytime someone wants to create a great mystique around business, (and) anytime they want to make it esoteric, they really don't understand what they're doing. There are four things you must do and I'll amplify each of them. You must (1) Get a great management team. (2) You must cut the cost. (3) You must define what business you're in. And (4) You must come out with a strategy for the future.[6]

In expanding point (4), he is particularly interesting.

> In addition to that, you really have to come up with a good strategy for the future, because if you just do the other things, you may get short-term results, but you have to couple short-term results with a long-term growth plan. You have to determine: How are you going to be a global competitor? What new products are you going to come out with? How are you going to make the business grow? What direction are you going to take with the business? These four points I think are amplified very well in my new book.[7]

If only he had followed his own words, he would not have contradicted himself. Dunlap's entire career, however, seems to have been built on a previously successful and singularly short-term strategy: Turn the company around, and sell it quickly. He is quoted in *The Wall Street Journal* as saying, "If you can't do it in one year, it isn't worth saving."[8] In the process of implementing this strategy successfully and spectacularly at Scott Paper, he amassed a personal fortune of at least $100 million, much of it in the form of stock options.

After the debacle at Sunbeam concluded with Dunlap's firing, a number of commentators have attempted a reasonable and balanced appraisal of his career, unlike many of his former employees and colleagues who have simply taken pleasure in bashing him. Edward E. Lawler, professor of management at the University of Southern California, may have summed it up best, when he was quoted in *Business Week*:

> The need to do a major downsizing is over (in most American companies). The opportunities to pick that kind of low-hanging fruit aren't as prevalent, and the second picking often requires different skills and methods than Al Dunlap is known for. Clearly, his era has come and is going.[9]

Yes, a new era in corporate management is emerging, yet it is not clear to even the most respected business analysts exactly what form it will take.

What's Wrong with Today's Leaders and Managers? Why Don't They Get It? Why Don't They Just Do It?

Late in the twentieth century, we have had several decades of experience with new and "revolutionary" business methodologies, such as total quality management or TQM, employee empowerment, restructuring and re-engineering, customer-focused organizations, and effective management in the information age. Each new methodology typically provokes intense interest, for a year or two, before we move on to the next one. We are currently deluged with a new wave of business books telling us how to lead and manage in the twenty-first century, including one by Gary Gardiner.

In the face of all these new methodologies, we are increasingly asked a couple of deceptively simple questions: What is wrong with today's leaders and managers? And why, with all the information we have at our fingertips, haven't we figured it all out and simply proceeded to manage brilliantly and successfully using the newest management tools and applications?

The questions are deceptively simple because the task of management is not simple. In fact, it is amazingly complex and difficult. Dunlap did not get it quite right. His single-minded approach to restructuring worked effectively in a single type of situation in a large and bloated company where fitful and halfhearted downsizing attempts had failed to turn things around, as was the case at Scott Paper.

If there were a simple, single, and successful way to manage, we would of course be doing it. For example, if we could succeed in the long term by focusing on customers—to the exclusion of everything else—we would simply do it. Many organizations that are currently successful, and say that they are solely or primarily customer- or stockholder-focused, have not yet begun to experience the problems that will inevitably occur as they travel further down the road. In many of these cases, the so-called Hawthorne effect accounts for much of their short-term success.

Almost Anything Will Work . . . Short-Term: The Hawthorne Effect Revisited

The Hawthorne effect is well known in the social sciences, but its implications have not always been fully understood in the field of management. Nearly 70 years after its discovery, let us revisit the phenomenon; it still provides valuable insight into why almost anything will work in the short run, including the latest management fad or theory.

The Hawthorne studies were carried out between 1924 and 1932 in the Hawthorne Works Plant of the Western Electric Company, by Elton Mayo and a group of researchers from Harvard University.[10] Mayo and his colleagues wanted to know what physical conditions in the plant, including such factors as noise and illumination levels, would increase employee productivity, and they designed a series of experiments to test such conditions.

The most famous of the Hawthorne studies are the illumination-room experiments, carried out between 1924 and 1926, where lighting conditions were manipulated as a group of workers assembled telephones and telephone components. When company engineers increased the intensity of illumination, productivity went up. This result led them to reduce lighting levels in order to determine what effect on production lower levels of illumination would have. As levels were lowered, productivity went up. As lighting levels were lowered still further, until the workers were toiling in virtual darkness, productivity was maintained at amazingly high levels. In the words of contemporary researchers Manfred Moldaschl and Wolfgang Weber: "Astonishingly enough, some of the assembly workers were able to maintain their degree of productivity when illumination was reduced to the intensity of moonlight."[11] This paradoxical result, which also occurred when other working conditions were changed, fascinated Mayo and the others because it had no obvious explanation.

Interviews with the workers began to reveal the actual cause. Employees were excited to be taking part in the experiment, because they were receiving friendly attention from the experimenters as well as from their coworkers. They were proud to be involved in the research. It was these social and psychological factors that accounted for the increase in productivity. The working conditions had little or nothing to do with the results.

The Hawthorne studies were responsible for the development of a whole new school of management, the human-relations school, which argued that helping, supporting, and encouraging workers was far more effective than using fear to motivate them. Perhaps even more important, they also showed that what we think is causing a phenomenon may not be the actual cause. The term *Hawthorne effect* has therefore become synonymous with a spurious or erroneous result, particularly in the short term.

In the long term, the workers assembling telephones in near darkness would probably have gone blind—not a good recipe for long-term worker satisfaction and productivity. This important aspect of the Hawthorne studies has not been as well assimilated and understood as the insight that research in the social sciences must be designed carefully to account for such spurious factors.

Generally, when a company adopts a new management tool or theory, whether it is re-engineering or total quality management, short-term gains in productivity and profitability often result. Many of these gains are undoubtedly the result of workers and managers being happy to be involved in an interesting and promising new experiment. Yet there is the tendency to believe that the marvelous developments are the result of the magical new managerial potion. Careful research is rarely or never done.

In popular language, everyone is *gung ho*. Gung ho, that is, until six months or a year have gone by and reality begins to sink in, reality in the form of a return to more normal or even lower levels of productivity.

So How Do You Make It Stick? The Achievement of Long-Term Results

The long-term effect of the adoption of new management miracles, not surprisingly, is cynicism and disillusionment, particularly on the part of employees. And often it is the new CEOs of publicly traded companies, perhaps assuming that they must make a big splash or they will be soon be history, who are vulnerable to the search for a quick fix or a flavor-of-the-month. John Byrne of *Business Week* has written a very perceptive piece on this topic under the title "Management Theory—or Fad of the Month?"

> Many theories degenerate into little more than fads because they appear to be quick fixes for a topical problem. The boss hears a fast-talking guru or reads about the latest fashion, and then orders his executives to look into it. They do, and before you know it, the company sends hundreds of managers off to seminars and hires consultants to make it happen. Yet chasing the latest fads risks undermining the confidence of employees who begin to greet every new buzzword with increasing skepticism.[12]

Whether the latest miracle is restructuring, downsizing, re-engineering, or empowerment, the employees become permanently cynical, as do the managers and executives charged with implementing it. Henry Mintzberg, in an eloquent article in *Harvard Business Review* entitled "Musings on Management," discusses the same phenomenon: Buzzwords and fads can actually make problems worse.

The buzzwords are the problem, not the solution. The hot techniques dazzle us. Then they fizzle. *Total quality management* takes over, and no one remembers *quality of work life*—same word, similar idea—no less, the craze not very long ago. How come quality of work life died? Will TQM suffer a similar death? Will we ever learn anything? Will anyone care?[13]

In the same article, Mintzberg also notes that healthy and smart organizations tend to stay off the bandwagon and steer clear of the fads. He focuses on re-engineering, a management tool that was popular in the early and mid-1990s. The premise of re-engineering is that over time, traditional companies—that is, companies that are functionally organized or vertical—tend to become bureaucratized, with internal organizational politics taking precedence over the company's performance. When the company is re-engineered, work systems are based on business processes or products, and information technology is used to increase the firm's productivity by breaking down or skirting the functional and bureaucratic barriers. However, as Mintzberg notes, in many cases re-engineering simply has not worked after a relatively short love affair and the Hawthorne effect. Instead, it has produced extremely high levels of fear in the companies that have adopted it, and actually lowered productivity in some cases.

Business Week columnist John Byrne and Henry Mintzberg agree that companies that jump on the management-fad bandwagon waste time, energy, and resources that could be better utilized elsewhere. Byrne comments that "smart companies tend to customize ideas, win top-down support for them, and devote considerable effort to making them work." In the same column, he also remarks that "limited attempts at using new techniques tend to produce poor results, regardless of the concept."[14] In "Musings on Management," Mintzberg is even more blunt and to the point: "Why don't we just stop re-engineering and de-layering and restructuring and decentralizing and instead just start thinking."[15] The necessity to start thinking, to think well, and to think things through is a vital ingredient in the philosophy of Value Driven Management.

True Success Is Creating Real Value Over Time

While we sometimes use the term "value" in a casual way to mean an individual's net worth, or the market value of a corporation's stock, just a few moments of reflection tell us that value is far more than just a financial concept. Bill Gates has tremendous personal wealth, for example, but Pablo Picasso may have been every bit as or more valuable to the human race—just ask any art lover, including Bill Gates. People love and value their pets, particularly dogs and cats, far beyond any possible monetary expression.

When CNN advises us that the average American family spends about $14,000 on its pet dog during the canine's lifetime, we are somehow not really shocked. Some things are worth more than money. Indeed, when corporations—those cold legal entities—are bought and sold, they are worth more than just money. They also have significant social value as well as other "intangible values." The terms *value* and *values* are multifaceted, and include not only economic values, but social, political, aesthetic, religious, and intellectual values, just to name a few.[16] In Value Driven Management, we use value in this broader way, and as we continue elaborating its philosophy, it will become clear that the concept of value and values is a complex and broad-based one indeed.

Thus, true organizational and personal success involves creating and maximizing value over time (VOT), including monetary or economic value, and incorporates a long-term perspective into the equation. The concept of VOT will be discussed in detail in Chapter 3. There are three premises regarding value and value creation that are vitally important components of Value Driven Management:

1. What we value drives our actions. What we value underlies everything that we do as human beings, including how we make decisions, what actions we take, and how we react to the decisions and actions of others.

2. Personal value structures are nearly always complex and interrelated. All of us have developed and refined what we value over the course of our lifetimes, and while some of the things we

value are more dominant than others, all of what we value is usually highly interrelated.

3. Some of the things we value are in congruence, while with others there may be conflict. Almost every decision we make, or action we take, is the result of some degree of interaction among what we value in a decision-making process that is unique. Most decisions represent an attempt to balance what we personally value, and to maximize congruence among what things we value. Value conflict in decision making is sometimes inevitable, both at a personal and organizational level, however, particularly when monetary or economic values are involved.

Recognition of the Power of a Value-Driven Decision-Making Process Is the First Step: The Value Creation Equation

The goal of Value Driven Management is for all its leaders and managers—and all of the individuals in it—to make decisions and to take actions that maximize the long-term good of the organization. To accomplish this, we believe that we need to understand the eight value drivers that impact virtually every organizational decision we make, and nearly every personal one as well, and how each value driver combines and interacts with others set in the value-creation equation. This interaction involves a balancing act that is sometimes mostly conscious, sometimes partly unconscious, usually subjective, but always an act requiring an intricate process of juggling, trading-off, and careful thinking before decisions are made and actions taken.

If this value-driven philosophy is understood and applied at every organizational level, it can fundamentally change the way organizations are managed and led in three breakthrough ways.

First, the systematic use of Value Driven Management will help *develop proactive patterns of behavior on the part of the organization and among all its decision makers* (as described in Figure 2-1, "A Continuum of Managerial Problem-Solving Styles"). *Proactive* organizations and people think ahead, anticipate problems, accept change as a fact of life, are not fooled by quick fixes and

Figure 2-1   A continuum of managerial problem-solving styles.

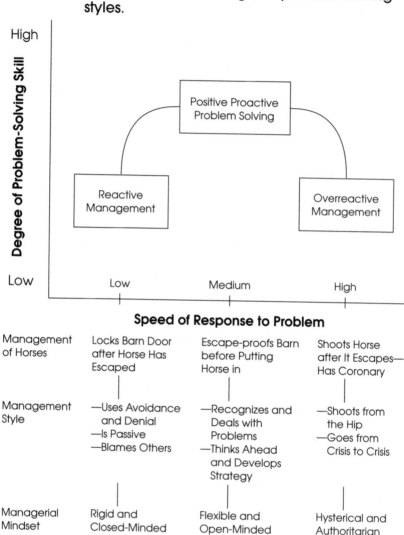

Management of Horses	Locks Barn Door after Horse Has Escaped	Escape-proofs Barn before Putting Horse in	Shoots Horse after It Escapes— Has Coronary
Management Style	—Uses Avoidance and Denial —Is Passive —Blames Others	—Recognizes and Deals with Problems —Thinks Ahead and Develops Strategy	—Shoots from the Hip —Goes from Crisis to Crisis
Managerial Mindset	Rigid and Closed-Minded	Flexible and Open-Minded	Hysterical and Authoritarian

Source: Adapted from Gardiner, 1996

magic bullets, treat problems as a way to grow and learn, are honest and ethical in their dealings with others, and look at the future as a source of opportunities. Employees tend to be organized around project teams and work processes, rather than in functional departments or a vertical hierarchy, and have developed a high degree of problem-solving skill compared to other types of organizations, as Figure 2-1 demonstrates graphically.[17]

On the other hand, *reactive* organizations are often lumbering and bureaucratic, depend heavily on formal authority, and generally spend a lot of time putting out fires because they failed to anticipate the "hot spots" or problems. They have trouble dealing with the rigors of market-driven economies and the accelerating pace of change.

Overreactive organizations are run by authoritarian managers and executives, and are often unethical and abusive. They often follow one of the oldest management precepts: "When in danger, or in doubt, run in circles, scream and shout." Any degree of stress brings out the worst in them, and they are never far removed from stress because, like reactive organizations, they usually fail to anticipate problems.

Second, the value-driven philosophy is designed to *develop effective and value-driven leadership at every level in the organization.* Again and again, as we analyze the decision-making and leadership styles of effective business leaders, we find that they are value-driven men and women who create value for their organizations that goes far beyond mere stockholder value. This is not to suggest that they have lost sight of profitability as an important corporate goal, but it is instead to state that the financial bottom line—as a value—is integrated with other value drivers in their leadership behavior. Value Driven Management and value-driven leadership are interactive and synergistic. Value-driven organizations will tend to develop value-driven leaders, and value-driven leaders will create value over time for their organizations.

Third, Value Driven Management *maximizes organizational and individual value and growth over time when the eight value drivers are integrated into organizational processes and permeate the organization's decision-making and action steps.* This new value creation equation is our way of conceptualizing one of the highest levels of "win-win" outcomes in which individuals and their organizations are becoming more valuable and fulfilled, and continue to grow and prosper throughout their lifetimes. This view is especially significant in today's growing force of high employment, knowledgeable workers, and the concept of measuring and managing organizational knowledge as intangible financial assets.

The Eight Value Drivers: An Overview

We have previously referred to eight important value drivers that impact organizational and individual decision making. These value drivers are to some degree interrelated and overlapping, but in total they encompass the universe of the organization, combining the internal and external variables it must confront throughout its existence. The eight value drivers are:

1. External cultural values
2. Organizational cultural values
3. Individual employee values
4. Customer values
5. Supplier values
6. Third-party values
7. Owner values
8. Competitor values

When these value drivers are used systematically and properly in the company's decisional processes, and when their individual and collective impact is weighted and balanced in organizational decision making, the firm will create value for itself over time—particularly in the long run. Each value driver will be described in detail in subsequent chapters, but in this section we present a brief overview of all eight value drivers and how they contribute to a value-maximizing model.

Value Driver 1: External Cultural Values

External cultural values include all those values outside the organization that may have an impact upon it, beginning with the values of the community or communities it is located in, the values of the region or regions it does business in, country cultural values, country subcultural values and other relevant subcultural values, as well as global cultural values in the new world economy. The power of the external cultural environment to influence organizational decision making can hardly be over-emphasized, although in any given decision-making situation the influence of a particular set of cultural values may vary greatly.

A couple of fairly simple examples, which are also wonder-fully complex as we begin to analyze them, may help illustrate this point. Assume, in the first such case, that you live and work in a small community where the business you own is also located. You are in the process of cutting costs and, as such, you consider letting an employee go (yes, firing him!). The employee's perform-ance has been marginal at best for a ten-year period. The em-ployee is well liked by his fellow employees, however, and last year was elected to a two-year term as mayor of your community.

You value your personal and company's reputation in the close-knit community where you have lived for many years. You have always been a good corporate and individual citizen, been environmentally responsible (you installed pollution-control equipment in your plant years before the law required it), and donated generously to community charities. You are concerned that terminating the employee will harm your reputation, yet you are also concerned that his poor productivity will continue to set a bad example for other, more productive, employees if they see him continuing to "get away with it."

You heartily wish that you had been more proactive in man-aging this problem, because you have seen it develop for several years. You wish that you had been more "tough minded"[18] in coping with the employee, perhaps in the form of more honest performance appraisals, rather than the glowing ones the em-ployee received; perhaps in the form of counseling and coaching, or referral to your company's Employee Assistance Program (EAP); or perhaps in the form of a transfer to another position the employee had several times hinted he wanted. You wish you had taken appropriate action before it became a thorn in your side.

A second, seemingly simple example is drawn from the arena of global business. You are the owner of a small brewery in Milwaukee and you decide that the time has come to enter the British beer market with your Mighty Milwaukee Malt Liquor. You launch an advertising blitz in Great Britain with a series of television spots that stress how drinking your beer will make the average British consumer more independent, avant-garde, successful, and ruggedly individualistic. To your shock, the themes that worked well for you in American television ad campaigns fall totally flat in Great Britain, along with the sales of your malt liquor.

You discover several weeks later, when you are discussing your failed entry into the British market, that your marketing vice president had given you (and many months ago!) an executive summary comparing the cultural values that are effective for consumers in the beer industry in both the United States and Great Britain. She gently reminds you that she had highlighted the finding that British beer drinkers value affiliation, tradition, history, and eccentricity, and that she had proposed that you design your British television spots to stress these themes. You tell her, somewhat lamely, that because you were so busy and stressed out, you had not taken the time to read her summary and you had gone ahead with the same old spots that had worked for you in the past.

The two examples above highlight the importance of considering what we have referred to as "external cultural values" when making decisions and taking actions.

Value Driver 2: Organizational Cultural Values

It is probably a truism that every company has a unique organizational culture. The impact of an organization's internal culture on its decision-making and action processes can be great, and in some companies the culture can even be a powerful impediment to rational decision making and the management of change. IBM is a case in point. Under the strong leadership of its founder, Thomas Watson, Sr., the company developed a strong culture of fairness and equity in terms of treatment of employees, including a proud tradition of never laying off productive and competent workers. The company was not only hugely successful—its dominance of the mainframe computer market for over three decades is still legendary—but it was almost universally regarded as one of the best companies in the world to work for.

IBM hit the skids in the late 1980s, however, and one of the reasons for its decline, ironically, was the cultural mindset that it had developed: It was Big Blue, the leading world manufacturer of mainframe computers. The company was something less than proactive in anticipating the personal computer revolution, and when the mainframe market began to decline, it was left unprepared as it slid from haughty prosperity to financial catastrophe in a breathtakingly short period of time. At a time when the firm needed to cut costs, downsize, and get into new products and markets, its long-standing tradition of no layoffs stood squarely in the way. It is an interesting historical fact that IBM did not successfully carry out critically necessary changes until it brought in its first outside CEO on April 1, 1993. Louis Gerstner (a "cookie man," as he was sometimes contemptuously described at IBM, in reference to his prior career at RJR Nabisco) was not a prisoner of the traditional IBM culture and its staid mainframe and no-layoff mindset. It is probably safe to say that the company's organizational culture permanently changed, albeit not without great pain, following the onslaught of overdue changes and the arrival of an aggressive and dynamic new CEO.

In the earlier example of terminating an employee who is popular in a small community, your company's organizational culture may also have an impact on the decision. If your internal culture values fairness to employees, and if fairness includes attributes such as loyalty and longevity, then terminating the popular employee might well result in anger, resentment, and lowered productivity. However, such resentment might also be a short-term phenomenon, and in the long run other employees might accept that the decision was a wise one, especially if the terminated employee is replaced with a more competent and productive one, or if it is evident that the business itself is improving.

Value Driver 3: Individual Employee Values

We have already noted that employees of an organization arrive at the workplace daily with their own set of personal values, which often drive individual decisions and actions. In general, the more congruent employees' personal values are with the values of the employing organization, the more successful individuals tend to be in their personal and their professional lives.

Congruency in this important area is a major contributor to creating and maximizing value over time.

A major implication of congruency is the need for careful selection of employees whose personal values closely match those of the organization. A civil engineering firm that values precision and orderliness in the execution of its work would be wise to hire employees who share those values. A high-tech Silicon Valley firm valuing technical competence accompanied by a willingness to continue learning and to cope with rapid change, would do well by hiring workers with those credentials and values. And an ad agency doing highly creative commercials for its clients would help itself immeasurably by aggressively seeking out highly creative copywriters and designers. An organizational selection process based on congruent or complimentary values is a proactive strategy that can save a company millions of dollars in terminations and turnovers, and build value by maximizing the firm's human assets over time.

In the continuing example of terminating a popular employee, the personal values of other employees would obviously also have a bearing on the decision, especially if equity and fairness were among their major concerns. On the other hand, if they valued hard work and productivity more than protecting a coworker, they might readily accept the employee's dismissal. Sensitivity to and recognition of these values on the part of the decision makers will consistently result in better organizational decisions.

Value Driver 4: Customer Values

Probably no subject has been talked about more in the last decade than customer service. The most ancient cliché of market-driven economies, "the customer is king," has been repeated endlessly, and the expression, "it's a customer-driven world," has become a virtual mantra for managers at every level in every organization. All too often, however, the delivery of customer service falls short of what customers value and expect. With this, an important opportunity for organizations to build value goes down the tubes.

When we analyze the reasons why companies fail to produce

superior, or even acceptable, levels of customer service, we find again and again that the concept of providing good service is paid abundant and dutiful lip service, but actions demonstrate that it is not really valued in the firm. Employees are often not adequately trained in how to treat customers well and fill customer needs. Supervisors often have other priorities. Further, employee values are not congruent with this customer, which causes a lack of understanding of what a customer wants.

It is interesting to note, however, that the late Sam Walton, one of the most successful entrepreneurs in American history, understood well the importance of customers to the success of his Wal-Mart chain. He was once asked by a reporter how it felt to be the wealthiest man in America, and his reply was along these lines: "Young man, if I lose touch with what the American consumer wants, I won't be the wealthiest man in America for long." Until late in his life, and until Wal-Mart had become a huge and sprawling chain, he visited every store every year to stay in touch with customers and Wal-Mart associates. His visible, physical presence in the stores was a living reminder to every Wal-Mart employee how much Walton valued his customers. These values permeated his entire operation and they live on after Sam Walton, continuing to build value for customers, as well as for shareholders!

In the fictional example of the popular employee, customer values would clearly also come into play in making a decision whether or not to terminate him. As usual, the value-driven approach immediately produces a stream of questions: Does the employee have a vitally important and good relationship with your firm's customers? Will you lose key customers if he is terminated? Is he creating value for you in this area, and will his termination destroy value? If there is a negative impact, will it be short- or long-term? Or, on the other hand, will customers recognize that you have finally dealt with a long-standing problem, and support your decision and action? Will your decision pay off for your company in the long run?

Value Driver 5: Supplier Values

Traditionally, an organization's suppliers have been thought of in terms of their ability and willingness to deliver quality goods and services promptly and dependably, and in terms of the concessions they might be willing to make in the face of a buyer's demands. In many industries, contracts with suppliers were something of a one-way relationship, with a major buyer putting heavy pressure on its suppliers to accept contracts weighted fairly heavily in favor of the buyer. This is an area where Wal-Mart, in light of its enviable reputation in many areas, takes a curious turn, as its relationships with suppliers have been the subject of a number of highly critical commentaries.[19] Wal-Mart has been accused of negotiating "cutthroat" contracts with suppliers, involving major price concessions on numerous products, and causing suppliers to "roll over" and accept deep discounts in order to win the business of the nation's largest retailer.

Wal-Mart's behavior may or may not be justified in the discount retailing industry where profit margins are typically low, and where industry overcapacity (which may currently be as high as 50 percent) produces ferocious price competition among major retailers. Any smart retail chain has to protect slim margins, and Wal-Mart's behavior may be justifiable on the basis of the industry in which it competes.

In other industries, however, such as the automobile industry, where innovations such as just-in-time inventory management have now become standard practice, relationships between buyers and suppliers have become much more reciprocal, as the values and behaviors of suppliers are often critical to maintaining a smooth and continuous production operation. In such relationships, the supplier (often an entrepreneurial outsourcing firm) has significantly more clout in dealing with the buyer. We are thus witnessing the development of new organizational arrangements, such as partnerships and joint ventures, in which buyers and suppliers are in interdependent situations and must learn to cooperate closely and trust each other in order to build value. And as we shall note in several other places throughout this book, trust is a major psychological and organizational variable in the value-creation process because, among other things, high levels of trust reduce so-called agency costs, or the costs we incur in watching others we do not trust. Since these costs represent unnecessary overhead to a business, their reduction amounts to a direct increase in productivity.

As for the mythical popular employee, if he had developed a special or strong relationship with a key supplier or suppliers, his dismissal might result in short- and long-term problems for your organization, especially if the supplier had counted on him for special considerations in negotiating contracts.

Value Driver 6: Third-Party Values

Every business organization in the world must deal with third parties, particularly whenever a decision is made or an action is taken. The examples range from humble to grand, from paying attention to local zoning laws to negotiating a multimillion-dollar tax settlement with the IRS. In the academic world, in the course of developing excellent nontraditional programs in business for adult learners, we have learned to pay scrupulous attention to accreditation standards and criteria because, if we do not, we risk losing our credibility—and then our market! Enlightened business organizations, without exception, have learned that illegal and unethical business practices will destroy value in the long run, and so they not only scrupulously obey the law, they often go beyond what is legally required of them.

Take, for example, what Levi Strauss did when it was forced to lay off nearly one third of its American workforce in 1998 and 1999—including numerous plant closings in 1999—because of a declining market share in the garment industry. Although the company was very slow to see and react to the changes that were occurring in the garment industry, particularly in the casual-slack and blue-jean markets, it tried to do the "right thing" for the laid-off workers, since it has a long history of respect for business ethics, American labor law, and third-party values generally. The laid-off workers were paid for eight full months, or six months longer than the law requires, and each was given a $6,000 allowance for job training, necessary relocation, and career training.

Although Nina Munk, writing in *Fortune* magazine under the provocative title, "How Levi's Trashed a Great American Brand,"[19] attributes the firm's difficulties to failed utopian management on the part of CEO Bob Haas and three in-laws who together run the company, *interrelated* value drivers may also have contributed to the firm's misfortunes. It seems clear to us that the company failed, for whatever reason, to pay attention to an important value driver in the retail industry: changing customer preferences, particularly among the young. These were changes that other retailers like the Gap were quick to pick up on. Many of the jobs that were lost may well be permanent losses, as the company moves production overseas, but in the future some of the laid-off workers may be able to return to the company, economic conditions permitting, and they will probably be proud to once again be Levi Strauss employees, knowing as they do how well the firm treats employees in difficult times.

Increasingly in the modern era, employee terminations are followed by employee lawsuits, which many dismissed workers win when the employing organization is unable to adequately document its case. Such lawsuits may cost the unhappy ex-employer hundreds of thousands of dollars in legal fees, while the ex-employee happily retains counsel on a contingency-fee basis, and goes for broke, so to speak. It is increasingly imperative as we move into a new millennium that when an employee is terminated, including our mythical popular employee (if we choose to go that route), his dismissal must follow proper steps.[20] His poor performance must be documented, he must be counseled, and, if possible, be offered help to improve his performance. Appropriate and progressive discipline must be used, and no improper or discriminatory actions must be taken against him. Such actions are proactive in the best sense, and while they may not entirely eliminate lawsuits over terminations, they will greatly reduce them, as well as reducing the possibility that an angry former employee will "go postal" and return to the workplace with homicidal intentions.

Value Driver 7: Owner Values

The owners of an organization are the stockholders in the case of public and private corporations, the partners in the case of partnerships, and the proprietor in the case of sole proprietorships. Ownership values in business organizations are usually fairly clear: profitability, leading to a decent return on investment (ROI). In market-driven economies, businesses must be profitable in the long run if they are to remain in business, and this is simply a fact of business life. Ownership values are vitally important value drivers, naturally, but they come into conflict with other value drivers more often than any other set of values we have been discussing.

The issue of how ownership should be structured in the modern, mature corporation has become the subject of increasing debate in recent years. Some authors, like Jeff Gates in his book, *The Ownership Solution,* have begun to argue that unless ownership in contemporary corporations is significantly broadened to include employees at every level in the organization (as opposed to ownership almost entirely by investors), corporations will become increasingly disconnected from the personal consciences of the people who work inside them, and will simply serve as financial vehicles for passive investors.[21] Gates voices strong concern about the increasing gap in most modern economies, including the United States, between the *haves* and *have-nots*, and attributes much of this to the phenomenon of investor ownership. This issue of ownership values and structure is very important, and we will return to it at length in Chapter 5.

Owners are typically driven by a strong profit motive, and while this may not be the only motivation they have, it is almost always a powerful one. The case of the popular employee illustrates this as we continue to consider whether or not to terminate him. Do you as an owner want to keep an employee on the payroll who is not making a positive contribution to the financial bottom line of the company? On the other hand, especially if you are taking a long-term perspective in the matter, will the potential for disruption and lowered morale cost you heavily in terms of reduced profitability, and therefore outweigh the financial gain you hope to enjoy from increased productivity if you fire him now? It is not just a question of firing him or not firing him. For example, will employee-assistance counseling help him at this fairly late point in his career, and lead to increased productivity and profitability for the owners? Would early retirement and a negotiated severance package be a better option for the owners? Would the employee resign if this option were presented to him as a face-saving measure, accompanied by an appropriate financial package? Could you move him to another unit of the company where he would be more productive, and create value? In

Value Driven Management we rarely encounter cases that are open and shut. These cases require the careful consideration of value drivers in the context of Value Driven Management, as the seemingly simple case of the popular employee so powerfully illustrates.

Value Driver 8: Competitor Values

In our continuing search to create value for our organizations, and for ourselves, does it matter in the least what values our competitors have? Do their business philosophies and practices have an impact on us and the way we do business? It may not be obvious at first, but the answer to both these questions is a strong and unequivocal "Yes!" Yes, how our competitors create or destroy value for themselves can matter greatly to us, and yes, our competitors' business practices impact us every day we are in business.

Competitive analysis is a major topic of discussion in virtually every course on strategic management taught in business schools, precisely because competition is so important in market-driven economies. A number of analytic models have been developed, in fact, to gauge the nature and intensity of the competitive forces that exist within an industry. Perhaps the best known of these, and the easiest to understand, is the five-forces model of competition developed by Michael Porter of the Harvard Business School.[22] Porter believes that the state of competition in an industry will be the product of five forces:

1. Rivalry among the sellers in the industry
2. Attempts by competitors to win customers with substitute products
3. Potential entry of new competitors
4. Bargaining power
5. Leverage enjoyed by suppliers of inputs and buyers of the product

The accurate diagnosis of these forces is necessary for an organization to gain and maintain competitive and strategic advantages, and the process of diagnosis must be ongoing and continuous.

The presence of strong competitors represents both a threat and an opportunity to a business, to borrow one of the pet concepts of University of Nebraska strategic-management professor Lester Digman.[23] Companies that are value driven, proactive, and strategically savvy use the tactics of competitors as information in an analytic process to develop and modify new products and strategies. Wayne Callaway, the former CEO and Chairman of Pepsico, has a pertinent observation in this regard. "Nothing focuses the mind better," he says, "than the constant sight of a competitor who wants to wipe you off the map."[24]

In the globalized new world of business, where many of the old rules have gone by the boards, competitors are now often viewed as takeover targets, with potential mergers that will create value for both organizations. In this new environment, a former enemy can easily become your new cohort. The creative possibilities are many. Could the values of competitors have an impact upon our still-pending decision as to whether or not to terminate the popular employee whose fate has been hanging in the balance through eight rounds of analyzing value drivers?

The answer is a carefully qualified "perhaps." If one of your competitors became aware that you are about to fire this employee, and considered him a valuable source of industrial intelligence, you would risk losing him (and any "inside" knowledge that he possesses) to a competing firm, with potentially serious consequences. On the other hand, if his knowledge were so limited and generic that his loss to a competitor would cause little harm, this value driver would have little bearing on your decision.

No Value Drivers Are Islands in and of Themselves

The English poet John Donne observed many centuries ago that "No man is an island, in and of himself."[25] For contemporary organizational decision makers, the poet's wise words ring true. As we consider the eight interrelated value drivers, and as we begin to use them in the Value Driven Management process, we become increasingly aware that to a greater or lesser degree all eight value drivers may impact us in the decision-making process. It is the systematic use of these value drivers, and their conscious integration into our analytic-thinking processes, that give us a powerful philosophy of management for creating value for the organizations that we serve.

Case 2-1

Whole Earth Commerce and the Creation of Value

When Ray Anderson grew his carpet manufacturing company, Interface, into a billion-dollar-a-year business, he operated on a widely shared assumption that the purpose of a corporation is to earn a solid return for shareholders, and that it has a duty to comply with the law. Writing in *TWA Ambassador* magazine, Bennett Daviss chronicles Anderson's transformation into a more environmentally responsible, but still highly successful, businessperson.[26] During a business downturn in 1994, when Interface's stock price took a tumble, Anderson read eco-entrepreneur Paul Hawken's book, *The Ecology of Commerce*, which decries the wholesale squandering of natural resources, and outlines a plan for making businesses environmentally sustainable.

Like it or not, carpet manufacturing is a messy and polluting business, and Anderson's company was no exception. Hawken's book was what he called ``a spear in my chest''[27] and he immediately set out to make Interface an environmentally sustainable company.

> Anderson set out to make his corporation's 26 factories the world's first environmentally sustainable manufacturing enterprise—recycling everything possible, releasing no pollutants and sending nothing to landfills. ``We're treating all fossil fuel energy as waste to be eliminated through efficiencies and shifts to renewable energy,'' Anderson adds. Idealistic, definitely; unbusinesslike, definitely not.[28]

Daviss notes that Interface became 23 percent more efficient over a two-year period in converting raw materials into sales dollars, and the savings helped Interface win a 1997 contract to carpet The Gap Inc.'s new world headquarters building in San Francisco.

Is the business of business simply to do business, or should it also do good? Daviss argues that a good business must first do business:

> ``Our product, which is food and service, has to come first,'' declares Judy Wicks, owner of Philadelphia's White Dog Café, renowned for its social activism and progressive employee policies. ``If I'm spending too much time on community pro-

grams, then I feel I'm neglecting work-place satisfaction issues for my staff, and that may take away from the quality of our product. We are, first of all, a restaurant—which allows us to do other things.[29]

He quotes Bob Dunn, now president of Business for Social Responsibility, and formerly vice president of corporate affairs at Levi Strauss, who argues that each company must find for itself a balance between social responsibility and doing business, and that social responsibility, as well as globalization and the rise of information technology, require more sophisticated management.

Daviss' article contains several other examples of companies that have created value by successfully practicing what he calls ''whole earth commerce.'' In a highly publicized example, the owner of the Malden Mills factory in Lowell, Massachusetts, Aaron Feuerstein, kept all his workers on the payroll after the plant burned down during the Christmas season of 1995, until a new factory was built. There has been a significant rise in productivity in the new plant, and a two-thirds reduction in quality defects. Marriott International, the hotel chain, installed a 24-hour multilingual employee hotline staffed by trained social workers under the leadership of Donna Klein, director of work/life initiatives for Marriott, and succeeded in reducing employee turnover—a major problem in the hospitality industry—to 35 percent, which is roughly one-third of the industry average. Klein had discovered in 1992 that personal problems such as domestic violence and immigration problems were a major source of employee turnover, and that the hotline was an effective response to these needs. She is quoted by Daviss as saying that the hotline costs Marriott over $1 million a year to run, but saves more than $3 million in hiring and training costs.

In contrast, the Body Shop ran into trouble when it was discovered that its claims of buying products from rain-forest natives and its catalog covers promoting progressive social causes were nothing more than marketing gimmicks. In 1994, *Business Ethics* magazine ran an article that revealed that less than one percent of the company's raw materials were purchased from native peoples, and that its supposedly ''natural'' products contained large amounts of petroleum.

> The article also hinted that the corporation's well-publicized concern for social betterment was prompted as much by marketing aims as by conscience. After the public glimpsed the gap between rhetoric and reality, the company's stock prices plunged and sales slumped. . . . Since then the company has begun to recover, matching its actions and rhetoric more closely.[30]

Bennett Daviss documents the decline and fall of another company, Consumers United Insurance Company, that got into trouble because it tried to do *too much* good and found itself insolvent as the result. Founder Jim Gibbons ran the company as a democracy: Employees had full ownership of the firm, and controlled company policy. The pay structure was sufficiently generous that even the lowest-paid workers could support a family of four. The firm did other good deeds: It bought 26 vacant acres in Washington, D.C., and built low-income housing on the site, and it also founded a youth group and promised the members that if they stayed drug-free and did not father children out of wedlock the company would pay for their college educations.

Consumers United was incorporated in the state of Delaware, and insurance regulators in that state became concerned that the company was not maintaining sufficient cash reserves to meet future claims. Its big-heartedness had essentially left it broke, and regulators sought a court order in 1993 declaring Consumers United insolvent. The state then seized its assets, and shut it down.

Daviss quotes impressive evidence, however, that socially responsible companies generally do well financially:

> Returns for the Domini 400 Social Index—a roster of 400 publicly traded, socially responsible firms tracked by the Boston investment advisory firm of Kinder, Lydenberg, Domini & Co.—have outpaced those for the Standard & Poor's 500 for each of the last three years. In 1992, UCLA business professor David Lewin surveyed 188 enterprises and found that ''companies that increased their community involvement were more likely to show an improved financial picture over a two-year time period. A 1995 Vanderbilt University analysis found in eight of ten cases, low-polluting companies outperformed their dirtier competitors. And the U.S. General Accounting Office reports that employee stock-option plans and participatory management schemes hike productivity an average of 52 percent.[31]

Daviss concludes his analysis with a quote from the editor of *Business Ethics* magazine, Marjorie Kelly, who notes that social responsibility makes sense in purely capitalistic terms, as well as creating value in other areas of life.

Questions for Discussion and Reflection

1. Do you agree or disagree with Bennett Daviss' assertion in the case study that the business of business is business? Why or why not?

2. Analyze Ray Anderson's restructuring of Interface, his Atlanta-based carpet-manufacturing firm by considering which value drivers he weighed most heavily in his decision-making process.

3. Are there some value drivers that were weighed very heavily? Others which were less important?

4. Do you agree with Bob Dunn, former vice president of corporate affairs for Levi Strauss & Co., that social responsibility, globalization, and the rise of information technology requires more sophisticated management?

5. How did the Body Shop succeed in destroying value for the organization?

6. Would it be likely to engage in the same tactics again?

7. What basic and vital principle of running a business did Consumers United forget? Analyze its downfall in terms of how it weighed the eight value drivers in its decision-making processes.

8. "Our people are our most important asset." Analyze this hoary old cliché in terms of the behavior of Marriott International, as it is reported in the case study.

Exercise 2-1

A Study of Personal Values

Introduction

All of us bring a set of personal values into the workplace with us. Most of us probably have a fairly clear understanding of what we do and do not value, but most of us have probably never done a systematic self-evaluation of our personal values. The following exercise is based on *The Study of Values*, originally developed by Gordon Allport, Phillip E. Vernon, and Gardner Lindzey, which is far and away the most widely used measure of individual values. Discussion questions follow the exercise.

Directions

Each of the following questions has six possible responses. Rank these responses by assigning a 6 to the one you prefer the most, a 5 to the next, and so on, to 1, the least preferred of the alternatives. Sometimes you may have trouble making choices, but there should be no ties; you should make a choice.

1. Which of the following branches of study do you consider to be most important for the human race?
_____ A. philosophy
_____ B. political science

_____ C. psychology
_____ D. theology
_____ E. business
_____ F. art

2. Which of the following qualities is most descriptive of you?
_____ A. religious
_____ B. unselfish
_____ C. artistic
_____ D. persuasive
_____ E. practical
_____ F. intelligent

3. Of the following famous people, who is most interesting to you?
_____ A. Albert Einstein—discoverer of the theory of relativity
_____ B. Henry Ford—automobile entrepreneur
_____ C. Napoleon Bonaparte—political leader and military strategist
_____ D. Martin Luther—leader of the Protestant Reformation
_____ E. Michelangelo—sculptor and painter
_____ F. Albert Schweitzer—missionary and humanitarian

4. What kind of person do you prefer to be? One who:
_____ A. is industrious and economically self-sufficient
_____ B. has leadership qualities and organizing ability
_____ C. has spiritual or religious values
_____ D. is philosophical and interested in knowledge
_____ E. is compassionate and understanding toward others
_____ F. has artistic sensitivity and skill

5. Which of the following is most interesting to you?
_____ A. artistic experiences
_____ B. thinking about life
_____ C. accumulation of wealth
_____ D. religious faith
_____ E. leading others
_____ F. helping others

6. In which of the following would you prefer to participate?
_____ A. business venture
_____ B. artistic performance
_____ C. religious activity
_____ D. project to help the poor
_____ E. scientific study
_____ F. political campaign

7. Which publication would you prefer to read?
_____ A. *History of the Arts*
_____ B. *Psychology Today*
_____ C. *Power Politics*
_____ D. *Scientific American*
_____ E. *Religions Today*
_____ F. *The Wall Street Journal*

8. In choosing a spouse, who would you prefer? One who:
_____ A. likes to help people
_____ B. is a leader in his or her field
_____ C. is practical and enterprising
_____ D. is artistically gifted
_____ E. has a deep spiritual belief
_____ F. is interested in philosophy and learning

9. Which activity do you consider to be more important for children?
_____ A. scouting
_____ B. junior achievement
_____ C. religious training
_____ D. creative art
_____ E. student government
_____ F. science club

10. What should government leaders be concerned with?
_____ A. promoting creative and aesthetic interests
_____ B. establishing a position of power and respect in the world
_____ C. developing commerce and industry
_____ D. supporting education and learning
_____ E. providing a supportive climate for spiritual growth and development
_____ F. promoting the social welfare of citizens

11. Which of the following courses would you prefer to teach?
_____ A. anthropology
_____ B. religions of the world
_____ C. philosophy
_____ D. political science
_____ E. poetry
_____ F. business administration

12. What would you do if you had sufficient time and money?
_____ A. go on a retreat for spiritual renewal
_____ B. increase your money-making ability
_____ C. develop leadership skills

_____ D. help those who are disadvantaged
_____ E. study the fine arts such as theater, music, and painting
_____ F. write an original essay, article, or book

13. Which courses would you promote if you were able to influence educational policies?
_____ A. political and governmental studies
_____ B. philosophy and science
_____ C. economics and occupational skills
_____ D. social problems and issues
_____ E. spiritual and religious studies
_____ F. music and art

14. Which of the following news items would be most interesting to you?
_____ A. "Business Conditions Favorable"
_____ B. "Relief Arrives for Poor"
_____ C. "Religious Leaders Meet"
_____ D. "President Addresses the Nation"
_____ E. "What's New in the Arts"
_____ F. "Scientific Breakthrough Revealed"

15. Which subject would you prefer to discuss?
_____ A. music, film, and theater
_____ B. the meaning of human existence
_____ C. spiritual experiences
_____ D. wars in history
_____ E. business opportunities
_____ F. social conditions

16. What do you think the purpose should be for space exploration and manned space flight?
_____ A. to unify people around the world
_____ B. to gain knowledge of our universe
_____ C. to reveal the beauty of our world
_____ D. to discover answers to spiritual questions
_____ E. to control world affairs
_____ F. to develop trade and business opportunities

17. Which profession would you enter if all salaries were equal and you felt you had equal aptitude to succeed in any one of the six?
_____ A. counseling
_____ B. fine arts
_____ C. science
_____ D. politics

_____ E. business

_____ F. ministry

18. Whose life and works are most interesting to you?

_____ A. Madame Curie—discoverer of radium

_____ B. Gloria Vanderbilt—businesswoman

_____ C. Elizabeth I—British monarch

_____ D. Mother Teresa—religious leader

_____ E. Martha Graham—ballerina and choreographer

_____ F. Harriet Beecher Stowe—author of *Uncle Tom's Cabin*

19. Which television program would you prefer to watch?

_____ A. "Art Appreciation"

_____ B. "Spiritual Values"

_____ C. "Investment Opportunities"

_____ D. "Marriage and the Family"

_____ E. "Political Power and Social Persuasion"

_____ F. "The Origins of Intelligence"

20. Which of the following positions would you like to have?

_____ A. political leader

_____ B. artist

_____ C. teacher

_____ D. theologian

_____ E. writer

_____ F. business entrepreneur

Scoring

Step 1—For each question, insert your score in the appropriate space in Figure 2-2. Note that the letters are not always in the same column.

Step 2—Total the six columns.

Step 3—Place the total for each personal value in the appropriate place in Figure 2-2. Connect the scores with a straight line to form a picture of your overall value orientation [use Figure 2-4]. See the example in Figure 2-3.

Interpretation

A description of each personal value is as follows:

- *Theoretical* The primary interest of the theoretical person is the discovery of truth. In the lab, in the library, and in personal affairs,

Example:

A __2__   B __6__   C __4__   D __5__   E __3__   F __1__

Figure 2-2 Personal value score.

Scoring Question	I	II	III	IV	V	VI
1.	A ____	E ____	F ____	C ____	B ____	D ____
2.	F ____	E ____	C ____	B ____	D ____	A ____
3.	A ____	B ____	E ____	F ____	C ____	D ____
4.	D ____	A ____	F ____	E ____	B ____	C ____
5.	B ____	C ____	A ____	F ____	E ____	D ____
6.	E ____	A ____	B ____	D ____	F ____	C ____
7.	D ____	F ____	A ____	B ____	C ____	E ____
8.	F ____	C ____	D ____	A ____	B ____	E ____
9.	F ____	B ____	D ____	A ____	E ____	C ____
10.	D ____	C ____	A ____	F ____	B ____	E ____
11.	C ____	F ____	E ____	A ____	D ____	B ____
12.	F ____	B ____	E ____	D ____	C ____	A ____
13.	B ____	C ____	F ____	D ____	A ____	E ____
14.	F ____	A ____	E ____	B ____	D ____	C ____
15.	B ____	E ____	A ____	F ____	D ____	C ____
16.	B ____	F ____	C ____	A ____	E ____	D ____
17.	C ____	E ____	B ____	A ____	D ____	F ____
18.	A ____	B ____	E ____	F ____	C ____	D ____
19.	F ____	C ____	A ____	D ____	E ____	B ____
20.	E ____	F ____	B ____	C ____	A ____	D ____
TOTALS:	____	____	____	____	____	____

the purpose of the theoretical person is to know the truth above all other goals. In the pursuit of truth, the theoretical person prefers a cognitive approach, one that looks for identities and differences, as opposed to the beauty or utility of objects. This person's needs are to observe, reason, and understand. Because the theoretical person's values are empirical, critical, and rational, this person is an intellectual and frequently is a scientist or philosopher. Major concerns of such a person are to order and systematize knowledge and to discover the meaning of existence.

   • *Economic*   The economic person is interested in what is useful. Based originally on the satisfaction of bodily needs and self-preserva-

Figure 2-3 Example: Personal value orientation.

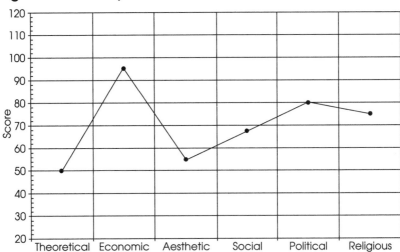

Figure 2-4 Your personal value orientation.

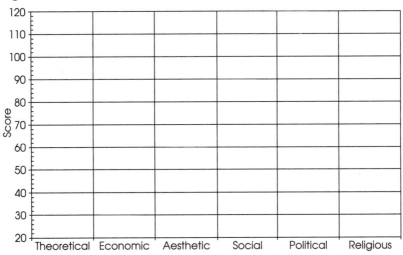

tion, the interest in utilities extend to the practical affairs of the business world: the production and marketing of goods, and the accumulation of wealth. This type of person is enterprising and efficient, reflecting the stereotype of the average business person. Economic values sometimes come into conflict with other values. The economic person wants education to be practical and regards unapplied knowledge as wasteful. Great feats of engineering and application result from the demands economic people make on people in science. Economic values may conflict with aesthetic values, such as in the advertising and promotion of products and services, except when art meets commercial ends. In relationships with people, the economic person is more likely to be interested in surpassing others in wealth than in dominating them politically or in serving them socially.

  ▪ *Aesthetic*   The aesthetic person finds highest satisfaction in form, harmony, and beauty. The value of each single experience is judged from the standpoint of grace, symmetry, and fitness. The aesthetic person regards life as a procession of events, with each impression to be enjoyed for its own sake. An aesthetic person may not be a creative artist; the aesthetic person finds chief interest in the artistic episodes of life. Unlike the theoretical person, the aesthetic person usually chooses, with the poet John Keats, to consider truth as equivalent to beauty, or agrees with H. L. Mencken, "To make a thing charming is a million times more important than to make it true." In the economic sphere, the aesthetic often sees the process of manufacturing, advertising, and trade as a destruction of important aesthetic values. In social affairs, the aesthetic may be said to be interested in people, but not necessarily in their welfare. The aesthetic person tends toward individualism, self-sufficiency, and idealism in personal relations.

  ▪ *Social*   The highest value for this type of person is love. The altruistic or philanthropic aspect of love is the interest of the social person. A humanist by nature, the social person prizes other people as ends in and of themselves, and not as tools or means to other goals. Therefore, the social person is kind, sympathetic, and helpful toward others. Such a person may find the economic and politic values to be cold and inhuman. In contrast to the political type, the social person regards love instead of power as the most suitable form of human relationship. In purest form, social values are totally unselfish.

  ▪ *Political*   The political person is interested in power and influence, although the person's activities may not fall within the narrow field of politics. Whatever the vocation, the political person seeks to be a "Machtmensch," an individual who is powerful. Leaders in any field usually will have a high interest in power and status. Because competition and struggle play a large part in all of life—between the sexes, between groups, between nations, and between individuals—many philosophers have viewed power as the most universal and the most fundamental of human motives. In certain people, however, the desire for direct expression of power is uppermost, and their primary values are social influence and the exercise of authority.

  ▪ *Religious*   The highest value of this type of person is spiritual peace. A religious person may or may not belong to an organized religion; people are religious if they but seek to comprehend the cosmos as a whole and to relate themselves to its embracing totality. Religious people have as their goal the creation of the highest and most satisfying value experience. Some people who are religious focus on events, people, and experiences in this world; that is, they experience meaning in the affirmation of life and active participation therein. With zest and enthusiasm, they see something divine in every event. On the other hand, some religious people are transcendental mystics, seeking to unite themselves with a higher reality by drawing from life. This type is ascetic and, like the holy men of India, finds inner peace and unity through self-denial and meditation. In many individuals, the affirmation and negation of human existence alternate to yield the greatest value satisfaction.

In evaluating your personal values, you should remember the following points:

- All six values on the questionnaire are positive.
- The questions do not measure negative values, such as greed or violence.
- Culture influences personal values. Through the processes of imprinting, modeling, and socialization, you learn to place higher importance on some values over others. Thus, the prestige afforded by the monarch, priest, businessman, scientist, artist, and teacher depends on the values of each society. In the Pygmy culture, the male with the greatest social esteem usually is not the strongest, wealthiest, most spiritual, most artistic, or most intelligent; rather, he is the one who shares most generously. Consider American society: What are the primary values for males in the United States today? Are they the same for females? Are they your personal values?
- By forcing choices among six personal values, the questionnaire gives an overall value orientation. This means that your lowest personal value may be more important to you than the highest personal value another individual holds. Similarly, your highest may be less important to you than the lowest of another individual. The questionnaire measures the relative strength of six personal values, so that you obtain a picture of *your* overall value orientation, or an understanding of what is most important to you.

Copyright © by George Manning and Kent Curtis. Reproduced with permission.

Different organizations reflect different values, and each organization's success depends on having people in it, especially leaders, who promote its mission. Some people may be ideally suited for theoretical organizations such as universities, economic organizations such as corporations, aesthetic organizations such as performing groups, social organizations such as social service agencies, political organizations such as political parties, or religious organizations such as churches, synagogues, and mosques. Obvious mismatches would be the social person who gives away the store and the person who uses religious position for personal power. Consider your own personal values. Ask yourself what type of organization, if any, would be most appropriate for you.

Questions for Discussion and Reflection

1. Based on your personal value orientation, have you chosen the right career path? Is there more than one career or occupation that might prove satisfying for you?

2. In view of your personal value orientation, are you working for the right employer? How congruent are your personal values with those of your employer? Your colleagues at work?

3. Do you agree with the authors of *The Study of Values* that economic values create more conflict, and lead to more incongruence, than any other set of values?

Endnotes

1. Albert J. Dunlap, *Mean Business* (New York: Simon & Schuster 1996).
2. John A. Byrne, "How Al Dunlap Self-Destructed," *Business Week*, 6 July 1998, 58–65.
3. Ibid., 59.
4. Ibid., 60.
5. Ibid., 59.
6. Ellen M. Heffes, "Blueprint For Radical Change If You Mean Business: Four Simple Rules—An Interview With Albert J. Dunlap," *Bisk Audio Financial Accounting Report*, April 1997, 2.
7. Ibid., 2–3.
8. James R. Hagerty and Martha Brannigan, "Inside Sunbeam, Rain-

drops Mar Dunlap's Parade," *The Wall Street Journal,* 22 May 1998, sec. B, p. 1.

9. Byrne, "How Al Dunlap Self-Destructed," 59.
10. Elton Mayo, *The Human Problems of an Industrial Civilization* (New York: Arno Press, 1977).
11. Manfred Moldaschl and Wolfgang G. Weber, "The 'Three Waves' of Industrial Group Work: Historical Reflections on Current Research on Group Work," *Human Relations* 51 (March 1998): 349.
12. John A. Byrne, "Management Theory—or Fad of the Month?" *Business Week,* 23 June 1997, 47.
13. Henry Mintzberg, "Musings on Management," *Harvard Business Review,* July–August 1996, 63.
14. Byrne, "Management Theory—or Fad of the Month?" 47.
15. Mintzberg, "Musings on Management," 65.
16. Randolph A. Pohlman, "Value-Driven Management," *Faculty Working Paper 97-01,* School of Business and Entrepreneurship, Nova Southeastern University, 1997.
17. Gareth S. Gardiner, *21st Century Manager* (Princeton, NJ: Peterson's/Pacesetter Books, 1996), 63–87.
18. Gareth S. Gardiner, *Tough-Minded Management* (New York: Fawcett Columbine, 1993).
19. Nina Munk, "How Levi's Trashed a Great American Brand," *Fortune,* 12 April 1999, 82–90.
20. Gardiner, *Tough-Minded Management.*
21. Jeffrey R. Gates, *The Ownership Solution* (Reading, MA: Addison-Wesley, 1998).
22. Michael Porter, "What Is Strategy?" *Harvard Business Review,* November–December 1996, 61–78.
23. Lester A. Digman, *Strategic Management: Concepts, Processes, Decisions,* 5th ed. (Houston: Dame Publications, 1998).
24. Wayne Callaway, as quoted in Arthur A. Thompson, Jr. and A. J. Strickland III, *Strategic Management,* 10th ed. (New York: McGraw-Hill, 1998), 68.
25. John Donne, *Devotions,* 17, as quoted in: http://www.campus.bt.com/CampusWorld/org664/quotez/740.htm (November 1998).
26. Bennett Daviss, "Whole Earth Commerce," *TWA Ambassador,* May 1998, 36–41.
27. Ibid., 38.
28. Ibid.
29. Ibid., 41.
30. Ibid., 40.
31. Ibid., 39.

Chapter 3

Enlarging and Clarifying the Concept of Value Over Time

Far too many business people, particularly in the United States, see the maximization of shareholder wealth as the sole purpose of a firm's existence. The widely used discount cash flow model of net present value (NPV) is an important financial model, and must be clearly understood if we are to develop the concept of VOT. NPV is simply not sufficient, however, to explain the broader notion of VOT that is inherent in Value Driven Management. This chapter explores a much broader, sometimes subjective, but (we believe) better way of understanding and analyzing the purpose of organizations, including privately held and publicly owned companies.

Most of us, including the majority of Americans, appreciate the fact that life is about more than just money. Even though we are sometimes accused, as Americans, of placing too much value on personal or corporate wealth, we also recognize the tremendous worth of other things in this earthly existence: spending precious time with our families, maintaining the beauty of America's still unspoiled natural regions, making charitable contributions or giving time to help others, and creating new products and ideas in our personal and professional lives, just to name a few. We may greatly admire Bill Gates because he is the wealthiest man in the country, but we also recognize that his company, Microsoft, has created tremendous value for America because of all the new and innovative software products it has created, along with thousands and thousands of jobs for working Americans.

Value takes many forms beyond simple monetary value, of course, although there is a great disconnect between the way in which we measure the financial value of the firm—the maximization of shareholder wealth at a given point in time—and the way in which we measure the *total* value of the organization, which includes such things as its human assets and intellectual capital, its sustainability over time as a business entity, its place in the community and the larger society, its creativity and resilience and flexibility, as well as its role in the creation of wealth in the society it serves. This latter and much broader definition of the value of the organization is in many ways inherently *subjective*, as opposed to the relatively simple and narrow financial measures of value.

Most of us do not charge out of bed in the morning and go to work solely because we anticipate maximizing our personal wealth, or maximizing the wealth of shareholders of our company. While compensation—especially *fair* compensation—may well be important to us, we are often equally motivated to perform well and create personal and organizational value because our jobs are creative and challenging, because we like the employees we work with, or because we love meeting the challenge of a determined competitor. While these latter characteristics of our employment are highly subjective, they are just as real and just as powerful as the simple and objective amount of the monetary compensation we know we will receive at the end of the month. The subjective and the objective are not in conflict, they are instead commingled.

In analyzing the true meaning of value over time (VOT), we must go beyond the merely objective or financial measures of value, develop new file folders and mindsets, and make sure that our categories do not get hardened. We must take a new and fresh perspective on the whole question of value, and what it means to create value over time. A necessary first step in achieving a new and broader perspective, however, is to make sure that we have a firm grasp of the traditional perspective of value. Thus, we will engage our readers in a straightforward review of the concept of net present value before moving on to a more multidimensional point of view.

Net Present Value (NPV) and Shareholder Value Maximization

Traditionally, the wealth maximization/shareholder value maximization advocates subscribe to the Net Present Value (NPV) model for evaluating how to make decisions within the firm to maximize shareholder value at a given point in time. The Net Present Value model, of course, makes the assumption that a dollar received in the future is not worth as much as a dollar received today (for a brief review of this, see Case 3-2 at the end of this chapter).

This means that to evaluate opportunities, we simply discount back future cash flows at the cost of using all funds (the cost of capital), and compare them in total to the cost at day one to undertake the project. This approach has two very basic problems for value enhancement, however, that stem from the same cause: dollar denomination. First, it refers to the net present value as though this were the only measure of value. However, value cannot just be measured in dollars of projected cash flows. Common sense tells us that value flow is much more complex than this. The value of family time, fun time, creativity, freedom, customer loyalty, supplier relationships, reputation with regulators, and so forth, simply cannot be measured with the NPV model since it can only deal with cash flows expressed in monetary terms. Second, the discount rate used is only for amounts of capital, and it is therefore also related to monetary units. This does not fit with a broader concept of value flows versus cash flows, even though economists talk about all of us having various discount rates that describe all of our preferences over time.

The NPV model could be used if the "V" really stood for value—more broadly defined—and the flows were truly value flows instead of cash flows, and if discount rates truly related to the preference of value flows over time. But of course this will not work even strictly to maximize shareholder wealth through share price maximization at any one given point in time. As this chapter unfolds, it will become clear why only using NPV and the traditional maximization of shareholder value at a point in time is not the complete answer to maximizing value creation for people and organizations. Why? Because it is too narrow and too simplistic!

When we are confronted with choices that are not purely financial, however, but which are *important* because they involve choices or clashes between important values, choices are not so simple, and are almost impossible to quantify. To illustrate this point, consider a situation in which a group of employees own a significant percentage of their company through an employee stock ownership plan (ESOP). In later chapters we shall discuss the fact that ESOPs can be a powerful means of creating value (as we use that term), but in this example, we are creating a somewhat simplified, and rather stark choice that companies sometimes face. Our fictional company believes it can improve its stock price by selling off two less profitable divisions, but in doing so, it will have to lay off several hundred employees, all of whom own thousands of shares in the company.

What to do? Should the company maximize its share price at a given point in time, or should it opt to retain the two less profitable divisions? Push has come to shove for the employees, and their choice will involve a complex and careful (and largely subjective) balancing act. If the share price went up dramatically as a result of the sale, and allowed them to retire and live in the community they love (with occasional trips to sunny Fort Lauderdale, Florida, of course), the improved quality of life they anticipate might well outweigh a reduction in their monthly income. On the other hand, if the share price increase projected is not "enough," they might prefer to keep their jobs and way of life and, of course, the two divisions. They might also ask themselves whether there is any guarantee that these two divisions will be viable in the long run. The plants in question require significant reinvestment if they are to be more productive, whereas a sale to a buyer now will produce immediate income. Many additional questions of this sort will undoubtedly occur to them as the decision process moves forward. The point is that the process itself will involve complex and multidimensional thinking, as well as highly subjective calculations of opportunity costs and an entire *stream of values,* all of which can be evaluated using a discount approach—but not one of which can be easily quantified or expressed in monetary units.

Some Thoughts on Risk, Rates of Return, and Ownership Rights

In the extensive literature that exists in the field of finance, there are hundreds of studies on the relationship between risk and rates of return on investment. A clear and identifiable bottom line unites many of these studies, which is that investors should earn a return commensurate with the amount of risk that exists in their investment . This common thread in research findings leads to an interesting conclusion when considering the creation of value, even when the perspective is financial. That conclusion is that optimization of return relative to risk is the appropriate criterion to use in evaluating investments, and not maximization of shareholder wealth at a given point in time. In a high-risk venture such as preliminary mine exploration in a remote western state, the rate of return may be phenomenally high (in the case of a major discovery of high-grade ore in an unexpected location, defying all geological logic), or it may be zero, as in the far more likely case of the mining equivalent of a "dry hole." Some investors may accept this risk, and their investment goal includes a sophisticated probabilistic analysis of a likely rate of return. On the other hand, if the investment is in a heavily regulated public utility that has produced dependable but modest earnings for decades, some investors accept that the rate of return, while steady, may also be lower. Both cases—high- and low-risk—lead to optimization of rates of return relative to risk as the most valid criterion for evaluating the investment, not maximization of shareholder wealth at a point in time.

There is another point of view on this whole matter that can be expressed in the form of yet another question: Who truly owns a publicly held corporation? The shareholders of record legally and properly own all of the physical assets of the corporation, and no one disputes this fact. When the question becomes, "Who owns the human assets of the organization?" the answer is by no means so clear and simple. Is the answer the shareholders? We think not. Human assets, of course, are precisely those assets that almost every corporation proclaims are their most valuable and upon which their major success depends. But, do the shareholders own these assets? It seems fairly obvious that each man or woman employed by the organization "owns" himself or herself. People are not property in any civilized society, even though people may work under contract for an organization. If we set out to maximize shareholder value using services owned by someone else—the very people providing them—are we now not involved in a highly complex balancing act and not a simple point in time share-price maximization solutions?

Our purpose here is not to pin our readers against the wall with arcane or technical questions, but it is rather to begin a true dialogue on what constitutes maximization of value, with the hope of embracing many apparently conflicting and diverse points of view. Political philosophers and economists from Adam Smith to Karl Marx have been arguing over such matters for centuries and usually from totally opposite points of view. Marx contended that labor should ultimately be the recipient of all wealth, because it is the source of the creation of all wealth[1] while Adam Smith argued with equal passion that the invisible hand of the marketplace in a free economy should distribute wealth.[2] History has come down somewhat heavily on the side of Smith, it seems to us, but it is not our purpose to judge the merits of the case made by either great historical figure.

The problem is that each figure takes a position that is a polar extreme and then with great passion attempts to persuade us with the truth of his views. The result is that rather than creating new knowledge through didactic reasoning, we get involved in a heated debate and end up clinging to and solidifying our own polar extremes. It is time to stop allowing the most articulate, the best funded, or the loudest voice to win the day.

Shareholders and other providers of capital deserve a fair and proper risk-adjusted rate of return on their investments in organizations, and employees deserve not only fair compensation relative to their ability to create value, but a decent working environment in which to create value. Suppliers deserve a fair price on the goods and services they provide the organization, and a relationship with that organization that is commensurate with the value of what they supply. The organization should engage in proper consideration of external culture issues, with due regard to what is valued by society. The firm should show appropriate concern for the view of third parties on what constitutes good business practices and just conduct, and the organization should recognize what its customers' needs and values are. It should also recognize what its competitors value in order to compete more effectively in a free marketplace.

If none of this sounds easy, it is not. When we broaden the conventional shareholder maximization model, however, to include the organization's entire stream of values, then these sorts of complex considerations arise again and again. Maximizing value using the value-stream approach represents a broadening and an enhancement of the cash-flow valuation approach, but its consistent use will also maximize long-term NPV for the organization. We admit that we do not have a single and simple formula as to exactly how value over time can be maximized, but this book represents a running start toward the successful implementation and use of the principles of Value Driven Management.

We might note at this point that the economic value added (EVA) model, which was originally developed by Stern, Stewart & Company, suffers from the same limitations as does NPV, even though EVA has become very popular among financial analysts and American corporations in recent years. Our purpose here is not to attempt to discredit NPV and EVA, nor to set up a debate between the proponents of NPV/EVA and Value Driven Management, but instead to broaden our perspective on what truly constitutes the maximization of value over time, even though we may not always be able to express that value in numbers or monetary units.

We are a society that loves numbers, and as Americans we have often been accused of attempting to put a number on just about everything we encounter in life. Some of our numbers are very good, but other numbers are just that, and may have little or no meaning. A corollary of our love of numbers is our suspicion that if something is subjective, it is highly questionable, invalid, or bad. Many of our subjective judgements are highly valid, of course, and some of our best judgements are those where we make subjective estimates of how a major decision may create value for us in our personal lives, particularly in the long run.

An example that the authors sometimes use in teaching the philosophy and principles of Value Driven Management in Nova Southeastern University's weekend MBA program (a far-flung operation with adult learners taking classes in more than 45 locations in several different countries) is a question that we like to pose to our students: Why did you make the choice to give up 18 months to two years of your normal life (if there is such a thing) to earn an MBA degree? The answers they give us are always well thought out, but usually highly subjective. It is especially interesting that they almost always feel that earning an MBA will create value for them in their personal and professional lives, and they have very little doubt of this. In many important respects, their judgments follow the logic of the NPV approach and they recognize that there will be significant opportunity costs, particularly in the short run, but that the long-term gains will outweigh the opportunity costs, making the MBA program a significant positive investment for them. The 18 to 24 months in which their family lives will be disrupted and during which they will sometimes be stressed out and exhausted, will be followed, they know, by an improved quality of life—financial or nonfinancial. When we ask them if they can put a number on it—either financial or nonfinancial—they simply smile at us with mild amusement. Their judgment that earning the degree will create value for them over the course of their lives is a sound one, and they know it.

This example of the foresight and good judgment of our adult students shows clearly that they have an intuitive and commonsensical understanding of the concept of maximizing *value over time* (VOT), which is one of the major intellectual underpinnings of Value Driven Management. VOT takes into account the short- and long-term consequences of a decision or an action, and attempts to link them together to consider the overall effect or ultimate consequences of a decision or action. We simply accept the fact that not all consequences or effects can be quantified, and we also posit that this is not important, since value creation can be meaningfully measured in subjective but valid ways.

VOT, as we use it here, is essentially the NPV of all future *value* flows. It is a methodology, we believe, that measures personal and organizational value creation and personal and organizational success, but not simply in terms of profitability or maximization of net personal worth. This is not to discount in any way the importance of organizational profitability in market-driven economies, or the importance of individual net worth, but it is a methodology that includes these measures in a larger and broader *stream of values*. Most proactive and strategic organizations and people have a commonsensical and sound understanding of this proposition, but may feel defensive about articulating it in a society that seems to worship short-term profitability and maximization of shareholder value at a given point.

A Multidimensional Perspective on VOT: Avoiding False Dichotomies

Randy Pohlman is a former professor of finance, and is very familiar with the paradigms and file folders used by financial analysts and economists. In discussing value over time, they claim that they understand that other factors—suppliers, customers, and employees—are important to the success of the firm over time, but in the final analysis they cling to their paradigms. To them, the value of the firm is simply shareholder wealth at a given point in time, and any additions to that wealth in the form of economic value added. The file-folder effect, accompanied by hardening of the categories, has struck again.

In developing the philosophy and the practices of Value Driven Management, we have learned that true value over time is much more than the traditional financial formulations would have us believe. These formulations can stimulate an analytic-thinking process that goes far beyond mere financial data. The point of the Value Driven Management model is to find the answers to how value is created and leave the measurement for now to NPV, EVA, or other models. Increasingly, management scholars like Peter Drucker and distinguished economists like John Kay (director of Oxford University's new School of Management Studies) are taking a multidimensional view of organizations. In an interview with *Fortune* magazine entitled "Shareholders

Aren't Everything" (which is summarized at the end of this chapter), Kay responded thusly to two questions posed by *Fortune*'s Erin Davies:

DAVIES: Is the primary purpose of management to maximize shareholder wealth?

KAY: Economists tend to believe that everyone acts to maximize something. But in our everyday lives, we aren't maximizing any particular thing; rather, we are balancing different and conflicting concerns. I think the same is true of companies, and therefore I don't think companies are there to maximize shareholder value—or social welfare. Managers of companies work to balance several different interests. That is the reality of how companies function.

DAVIES: What is a company's purpose, if not to maximize shareholder value?

KAY: Producing goods and services people want. Business is about providing employment, providing value for customers, for developing skills of employees, for developing capabilities of suppliers—as well as earning money for shareholders.[3]

Kay's answers to *Fortune*'s questions are particularly noteworthy because he brilliantly avoids a false dichotomy, namely that a business has to be on one side of the fence or the other—either on the side of creating shareholder wealth, or on the side of creating social welfare. There are undoubtedly many business people in this country who believe (à la Al Dunlap) that the maximization of shareholder wealth is the sole purpose of a firm's existence; but there are also a lot of people who believe that "profit" is a dirty word and that employers should provide all sorts of entitlements to their employees and the other stakeholders of the organization. Both sides are wrong, of course, because the real world is far more interconnected and complicated than these diametrically opposed views would have us believe.

Many of our so-called dialogues today are really what Peter Senge calls "discussions" in his popular book, *The Fifth Discipline*.[4] Senge notes that in discussions, as he uses the term, both sides take rigid, extreme, and polarized positions, and then attempt to show how articulate and brilliant they are by proving

the other side wrong. This type of discussion or debate wastes
time and energy in a lot of organizations, and impedes the creation of new knowledge because both sides end up more polarized than ever, still clinging rigidly to their original file folders.
Arguably, polarized discussions—whether over abortion, free
trade, or the true purpose of an organization—destroy value in
the long run because they divide rather than unite, and hurt
rather than heal.

The management guru Peter Drucker avoids such false di-
chotomies in an article in *Forbes ASAP* entitled "The Next Information Revolution," in which he argues that a new information
revolution is already well under way—a revolution not in technology, machinery, techniques, software, or speed, but in *concepts*.[5]
Drucker comments that the next information revolution is asking
two related questions: What is the meaning of information, and
what is its purpose? He notes, further, that the next revolution:

> . . . is forcing us to redefine what business enterprise
> actually is and should be. This largely underlies the new
> definition of the function of business enterprise as the
> "Creation Of Value And Wealth," which in turn has trig-
> gered the present debate about the "governance of the
> corporation," that is, for whom the business enterprise
> creates value and wealth.[6]

In the same article he goes on to remark that the new revolution
involves far more than preserving assets and controlling costs,
although these management tasks still matter.

> A serious cost disadvantage may indeed destroy a busi-
> ness. But business *success* is based on something totally
> different, the creation of value and wealth. This requires
> risk-taking decisions: on the theory of the business, on
> business strategy, on abandoning the old and innovating
> the new, on the balance between the short- and the
> long-term, on the balance between immediate profit-
> ability and market share.[7]

In short, according to Drucker, businesses must be smart and
proactive in order to succeed. Further, successful decision mak-

ing involves a balancing or juggling act among competing concerns or values. He points out that thus far, unfortunately, top management has used the computer and the data flow it makes possible to focus *inward* in what Drucker calls a degenerative way (or in our language, in a way that does not create value) on costs and efforts rather than to focus *outward* on opportunities, changes, and threats (or in a strategic and proactive way that will create value for the firm).

A Value-Driven Decision-Making Model

In the process of decision making and in the course of taking the subsequent actions that flow from their decisions, organizations and individuals naturally (but often subconsciously) go through a series of analytic steps as they begin to consider the impact of the actions they contemplate taking. There are huge individual and organizational differences, not surprisingly, in the depth, breadth, and overall quality of this analytic process, but the rudiments of it are fairly similar for all of us.

The two key elements in value-driven decision making are deceptively simple: knowing what the organization or individual values and how they should be prioritized, and knowing the relevant or appropriate time horizon. Almost every organizational and personal decision comes back to *what that organization or individual values* in the short- and the long-term and, perhaps most importantly, to how value drivers interact in the decision-making process.

Time horizons for their part differ from situation to situation, of course, ranging from the 15-year commitment of First Union Bank (and many other American companies) for major capital purchases of cutting-edge technology; to the agonizing and surprising decision of Levi Strauss & Company in the late 1990s (and many other American firms) to lay off a significant proportion of its domestic workforce.

Time frames may also interact, and sometimes in subtle ways. For example, many American companies discovered in the mid-1980s that they were no longer very competitive with major Japanese firms like Sony and Toyota (which had already effectively implemented total quality management, and were lean and mean), which set in motion a short-term decision to begin downsizing and restructuring—a process that was often carried out hastily and sloppily and which generated a great deal of negative publicity for them. This short-term process often led, however, to a significant long-term commitment to improving quality and productivity, including significant reorganization and restructuring to position the company to compete more effectively in the global economy. The examples are many, but in the auto industry, the Ford Motor Company was proactive and an early starter, while in personal computers, IBM was slow and reactive and encountered major problems.

When American firms like Ford saw the light, they made a long-term commitment to organizational change, including a major investment in cutting-edge computer technology that has been a major factor in this nation's emergence as the world's unchallenged economic superpower in the late 1990s. The ability of this country to creatively scramble is still unrivaled, whereas its ability to be strategic and proactive is more questionable.

Interactive effects among value drivers and time frames are so common and complex in the value-driven decisional process that it is difficult to describe them simply, and a real challenge even to visualize them. In creating value over time, we *prioritize* values and time pressures, we *balance* competing value drivers and interests, we analyze the *impact* of the decisions and actions we are considering, and we do our best to *integrate* all these dynamic forces into a choice or series of choices that we think will maximize value for us and/or our organization, particularly in the long run. We have attempted to illustrate the value-driven decision-making model graphically in the chart that appears in Figure 3-1. It is a model that we will return to again, however, and in much greater detail.

Decisions That Create Value, Decisions That Destroy Value

In an ideal and platonic world, where each of us had the vision and wisdom to make decisions that we knew with great certainty

Figure 3-1   The value driven decision-making model.

Two Key Questions Initiate the Analytic Process:

1. What does my organization value, or do I value, and how should these values be prioritized in this decisional process?

2. What are the appropriate or relevant time horizons for me or my organization?

Leading to an analytic process including:

BALANCING OF COMPETING VALUES

ANALYSIS OF THE IMPACT OF THE DECISION TO BE MADE AND THE ACTIONS TO BE TAKEN, SHORT- AND LONG-TERM

INTEGRATION OF DYNAMIC FORCES INTO A DECISION OR DECISIONS AND AN ACTION OR ACTIONS

Leading to decisions and actions that will create and maximize:

VALUE OVER TIME

(VOT)

would maximize value for us and our organizations over time, we would of course do so. In the real world that we all live in, unfortunately, we are often faced with so many pressures—of time, of economic uncertainty, of great social complexity—that we sometimes do not visualize the platonic world of forms, ideals, and organizational and personal self-actualization with the immediacy and the clarity that we otherwise might. Stress gets in our way, and we feel that we are trapped in a cave and see only flickering shadows on the wall, but we still struggle to do our best to make wise decisions.[8] In developing the philosophy of Value Driven Management, we feel that we can better see a world where enlightened individuals and organizations consistently act in a way that enhances value for them, and the world they live in—if we carefully examine what it means to make value-driven decisions and analyze how effectively organizations make use of value drivers as they confront the complexity of their worlds. In the following chapters of this book, we will do our best to emerge from the shadows of the cave into a brave new world of forms: the world of Value Driven Management.

Case 3-1

Shareholders Aren't Everything: An Interview with John Kay

In the February 17, 1997, issue of *Fortune* magazine, in an interview with Erin Davies, Dr. John Kay—economics professor, author, founder and chairman of London Economics (a consulting firm), and at that time director designate of Oxford University's new School of Management Studies—argued vigorously in favor of a proposition that we have put forth in this book: that maximization of shareholder value is not the sole purpose of a firm's existence. Kay responded early in the interview with a somewhat rhetorical question to his interviewer, "Why should managers give priority to the shareholders' interests?"[9] In responding to his own question, Kay remarked that if a business consisted purely of its physical assets, then perhaps shareholders should have priority, but he then noted the business is far more than just physical assets: It has a history, a structure of relationships, and a reputation. These are things that allow the company to add value, "... and to say that shareholders own these things is kind of bizarre. They don't and they couldn't."[10]

In response to Davies' question whether or not the primary purpose of management is to maximize shareholder wealth, Kay responded with an answer that we quoted earlier: that the true purpose of a company is to balance different and conflicting concerns, and producing goods and services that people want. He takes a value-driven and multidimensional view of the purpose of business: "Business is about providing employment, providing value for customers, for developing skills of employees, for developing capabilities of suppliers—as well as earning money for shareholders."[11] In viewing the company as a community, he argues that the interests of all the groups who belong to the community must be taken into account—and balanced—if the firm is to flourish.

He notes that company managers might say, if asked, that they focus on maximizing shareholder value; but the way in which they actually *behave* is more in keeping with a stakeholding view of the company. He also notes that both American corporate law and capital markets virtually force managers to give priority to shareholders' interests, but that this is not true in countries such as Germany, Japan, and Great Britain. Perhaps the most interesting assertion in the entire interview is his contention that managers of American companies need to understand two points: focusing exclusively on increasing shareholder wealth may actually preclude management from doing things that are in the long-term interests of shareholders, and giving shareholders top priority may actually make it harder to maximize shareholder value in the long run, and may also prevent management from running the business in a way that everyone would agree would lead to better results.

Kay uses GE as an example of a well-managed company that has done things right for a long time—over 100 years. He argues that it has been able to do so because it has maintained its corporate personality, which he feels is the essence of any company, throughout its corporate history, and that it has been able to apply its personality to an array of changing businesses and changing environments. Its outstanding reputation has also enabled it to continue attracting extraordinary management talent, decade after decade, in exactly the same way that other outstanding companies like Caterpillar and P&G do. He concludes the interview by noting that in MBA programs, "Students need to understand that making commitments to stakeholders can be a source of competitive advantage."[12]

Questions for Discussion and Reflection

1. Do you agree with John Kay's statement that both U.S. law and our country's capital markets virtually force managers to give priority to shareholders' interests?

2. Kay comments that ". . . focusing exclusively on increasing shareholder wealth may preclude you from doing things that would actually be in the long-term interests of the shareholders." Do you agree with this statement?

Case 3-2

Net Present Value

For those of you who do not deal with Net Present Value (NPV) every day or have not yet been exposed to the concept, this case is a brief tutorial in the model. NPV is based upon the concept of "time value of money." In other words, we prefer a dollar today to a dollar in the future due to the fact that if we have a dollar today, we may be able to invest it wisely and have more than a dollar in the future.

The following example illustrates this point. Assume that you get $1.00 at the beginning of this year and you then invest it for three years at a 10 percent rate of interest. How much money will you have at the end of three years?

Year 1	Year 2	Year 3
$1.00 x 1.10 = $1.10	$1.10 x 1.10 = $1.21	$1.21 x 1.10 = $1.331

Compounding ————————————————————————————————→

Our example shows that at the end of year one you would have $1.10, at the end of year two you would have $1.21, and at the end of year three you would have $1.33. This simple example clearly shows the impact of the "time value of money" on *compounding* for future value.

Now assume that you will receive $1.00 *per year* for three years at the *end* of each year. This is typically what happens when we make an investment and receive cash flows in future years. What would you be willing to pay for this cash-flow stream, assuming that you could still earn 10 percent on your money? There are several steps involved in this calculation.

The first question is what is the dollar amount you received at the end of year one worth today? Or another way of saying it is, how much will it take today to have $1.00 a year from now at 10 percent interest? (See the diagram below to make this calculation):

Year 1	
$.909 x 1.10 = $1.00	i.e., $.91

←—————————————————   Discounting

What is the dollar worth today that you will get two years from now?

Year 1	Year 2	
(.826) 1.10 = $.9086	(1.10)(.909) = $1.00	i.e., $.83

←——————————————————————   Discounting

In other words, you should not be willing to pay more than 83 cents today to receive $1.00 two years from now since if you invested 83 cents today at 10 percent interest compounded, you would have $1.00 two years from now.

What is the dollar worth today that you get three years from now?

Year 1	Year 2	Year 3	
(.751) x 1.1 = .826	(.826) x 1.1 = $.909	(.909) x 1.1 = $1.00	i.e., approx. $.75

Discounting

Clearly, all you would be willing to spend today to receive $1.00 three years from now would be 75 cents, which you can invest at 10 percent interest, compounded, in order to have $1.00 three years from now. If we wanted to know the total value of receiving $1.00 one year from now, two years from now, and three years from now, on a present "value" basis, we would simply sum up the 91 cents plus 83 cents, plus 75 cents and realize that the present value per value of the cash flows is $2.49. Therefore, the most you would pay for a cash flow of $1.00 per year for three years, if you require a rate of return of 10 percent, would be $2.49.

If you only had to pay $1.50 to buy this stream of cash flows of $1.00 per year for three years, your net present value would be 99 cents. In other words, $2.49 minus $1.50. The Net Present Value model takes the present value of the future cash flows ($2.49) and subtracts the cost of them (i.e., $1.50) to get the net present value.

Let's now briefly look at a decision to invest in a machine that costs $10,000 today and returns $4,000 in cash flow each year for three years. Your discount rate (cost of capital) is 10 percent. Should you invest or not? The answer seems to be an obvious "yes." You get $12,000 and only invest $10,000. Looking more closely, however, and taking the time value of money into account, we see that it is not a good investment, as shown below.

	Cash Flow	Discount Factor	Present Value
Year 1	$4,000	.909	$3,636
Year 2	$4,000	.826	$3,304
Year 3	$4,000	.751	$3,004
Present Value of Future Cash Flows			$9,944
Minus Initial Cost			$10,000
Loss on Investment			$56

In other words, it is not a good investment to spend $10,000 for a piece of equipment that produces cash flow with a present value of only $9,944.

Questions for Discussion and Reflection

1. Does NPV, as it has been clarified in the examples found in this case, adequately measure an organization's *stream of values*?

2. If you were to rely exclusively upon immediate profit to measure creation of value, would it encourage good business judgment on your part; for example, would it encourage you to make a long-term investment in new capital?

3. Can you think of some new and innovative ways of measuring an organization's stream of values? Remember our admonition that *subjective* measures are often useful and valid.

Endnotes

1. Karl Marx, *Capital, a Critique of Political Economy* (New York: The Modern Library, 1906).
2. Adam Smith, *An Inquiry into the Nature and Causes of the Wealth of Nations* (Edinburgh: A. and C. Black, 1862).
3. Erin Davies, "Shareholders Aren't Everything," *Fortune*, 17 February 1997, 133.
4. Peter Senge, *The Fifth Discipline* (New York: Currency Doubleday, 1994).
5. Peter F. Drucker, "The Next Information Revolution," *Forbes ASAP*, 24 August 1998, 47–58.
6. Ibid., 47.
7. Ibid., 48.
8. Plato, *The Republic* (Harmondsworth, Middlesex: Penguin Books, 1955).
9. Davies, "Shareholders Aren't Everything," 133.
10. Ibid.
11. Ibid.
12. Ibid., 134.

Chapter 4

The Underlying Assumptions of Value Driven Management

A house without a strong foundation will not endure, and a house divided against itself will not stand. No great structure can be built upon a sea of shifting sands. Such time-tested and honored metaphors remind us that no sound and sensible philosophy of management can be developed that is not based on sound and sensible principles, and on premises that have withstood and will withstand the great test of time. The 11 underlying assumptions of Value Driven Management not only meet this criterion, we believe, but are also safely grounded in the principles and dynamics of market economies and the emergence of a globalized world.

In the process of developing the philosophy of Value Driven Management and discussing some of the decisional steps and business practices that support and help develop it, we have made 11 underlying assumptions. We feel that these assumptions are critical to our model and its success in the new world of business and management. We have already made reference to a number of them in several different places in the first three chapters. At this point, we will describe them (they are summarized in Figure 4-1), with the purpose of demonstrating how they support the concept of Value Driven Management, and how they help us begin to identify the business practices and organizational-development tools that are necessary to its successful implementation.

Figure 4-1   The assumptions of Value Driven Management.

- Assumption   I: Value creation is good
- Assumption   II: What is valued drives action
- Assumption   III: The creation of knowledge and its
                       appropriate use leads to value creation
- Assumption   IV: Value is subjective
- Assumption   V: There are value adders and destroyers
- Assumption   VI: Markets provide vital information
- Assumption   VII: Opportunity costs affect value
- Assumption VIII: Order is spontaneous
- Assumption   IX: Values can compete or be complementary
- Assumption   X: Any action can have unintended
                       consequences
- Assumption   XI: All employees are employees

Assumption I: Value Creation Is Good

The most basic assumption of Value Driven Management is that
value creation is good both for the individual and the organization for which he or she works. A corollary of this first assumption is that organizations that do not create value will eventually
cease to exist, and that people who do not create value for organizations will eventually lose their jobs.

We further assume that profits made *legally* and *ethically* are
good, and that they can fuel the creation of other values, such
as increased employment and an increase in the nation's gross
domestic product. *Illegal* profits are another matter, however.
Consider for a moment the billions and billions of dollars rung
up in illegal profits by the drug barons of Colombia and other
Central and South American nations. Are these persons not creating value, since they are clearly satisfying customer needs, largely
in the United States, and creating employment and production
opportunities for impoverished peasant farmers in South
America?

From the perspective of Value Driven Management, value
has not been created. The net effect of illegal drug profits, in fact,
is that some people have profited from value destruction. The
destruction of lives far outweighs the profits (value) created, and
most countries have recognized that fact. The cost of human pain

and suffering, corruption, and the other negative societal consequences of illegal drug use clearly represent a net negative *destruction of value*. It does indeed matter how money is made.

Honest and ethical profits are another matter. When money is made by giving legal customers the goods and services they want, value is created. When a profitable and growing business creates employment for working people, value is created. And when creative and innovative firms—like Microsoft, Southwest Airlines, or First Union Bank—consistently come up with new ideas (thanks to the intelligence and entrepreneurship of their employees), value is created. The financial foundation of free-market economies is profitability, and the psychological underpinning of all such economies is the profit motive. Enough said.

Assumption II: What Is Valued Drives Action

We sometimes feel that economists and psychologists cannot agree on anything, but the following proposition unites both professions: what people value drives their actions. Abraham Maslow's familiar hierarchy of needs supports the proposition from a psychological perspective. The basic concept in his hierarchy (which was popularized in his classic 1954 volume, *Motivation and Personality*)[1] is the idea that people must satisfy lower-level or basic needs first—basic physiological needs, the need for safety and security, the need to be loved—before they can move on to higher-level or growth needs—the need to love, the need for self-esteem, and the need to develop the creative potential that every person has.[2] The need hierarchy might not be as neatly sequential as the usual pyramid-like representation of it implies (see Figure 4-2), but it certainly makes sense that when people are starving and homeless, or when they are faced with losing their jobs in a major downsizing, they will be preoccupied with these matters and will value food, water, shelter, and income highly, and to the exclusion of other values. Basic needs are valued more highly in periods of recession, or in impoverished nations, naturally enough. Growth needs, on the other hand, become more valued and important in periods of relatively full employment such as the United States has been enjoying in the

Figure 4-2   Maslow's hierarchy of human needs.

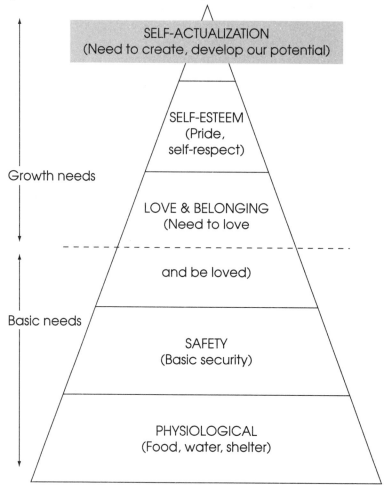

late 1990s, where employees (especially well-educated and highly skilled ones) have the luxury of looking for employers who will treat them well and jobs that are interesting and challenging and lead to a lifetime of learning and growth.

From an economic perspective, Ludwig von Mises used the field of praxeology, or human action, to study and understand values in a 1963 book, *Human Action: A Treatise on Economics*, that has also become a classic.[3] To differentiate praxeology from psychology, von Mises remarks that "the theme of psychology is the internal events that result or can result in a definite action. The theme of praxeology is action as such."[4] A rather lengthy quote from *Human Action* clearly makes the point that what is valued drives action:

> We call contentment or satisfaction that state of the human being which does not or cannot result in any action. Acting man is eager to substitute a more satisfactory state of affairs for a less satisfactory. His mind imagines conditions that suit him better, and his action aims at bringing about this desired state. The incentive that impels a man to act is always some uneasiness. A man perfectly content with the state of affairs would have no incentive to change things. He would have neither wishes nor desires; he would be perfectly happy. He would not act; he would simply live free from care. But to make a man act, uneasiness and the image of a more satisfactory state alone is not sufficient. A third condition is required; the expectation that purposeful behavior has the power to remove or at least alleviate the felt uneasiness. In the absence of this condition, no action is feasible.[5]

In his 1993 book, *The Armchair Economist*, Steven Landsburg puts the proposition another way and succinctly: "Most economics can be summarized in four words: people respond to incentives. The rest is commentary."[6]

Sears, formerly the nation's number one retailer, discovered to its dismay in the early 1990s that people do indeed respond to incentives. The huge Chicago-based retailer had been losing customers for years to aggressive discounters such as Wal-Mart and Target, and was desperately seeking ways to reduce costs and increase sales volume. In 1992 it cut the base salary of employees in its auto repair division, and established a system of bonuses based on volume sales. The hope was that linking pay to performance would increase efficiency and result in happier and satisfied customers; the result was a disaster.

Management authors Gareth Jones, Jennifer George, and Charles Hill offer a clear analysis of what actually happened.

Initial results of the new output control system seemed to suggest that it was working. Dollar volume of sales was up and so was employees' pay. Soon, however, a number of complaints were reported from disgruntled customers who believed that Sears' employees were recommending expensive and unnecessary car repairs. California's Consumer Affairs Department was one of the first governmental agencies to investigate these claims. It concluded in late 1992 that on 34 of the 38 undercover runs that the department had conducted, Sears' personnel had charged an average of $235 for unnecessary repairs. Sears' employees, having difficulty keeping their take-home pay at previous base levels, apparently were deceiving customers about the dollar amount of repairs that were really necessary.[7]

Not surprisingly, Sears scrapped the volume-based bonus system, but the damage had been done. A flood of litigation eventually led to an out-of-court settlement in 1992, which required Sears to pay damages to thousands and thousands of affected consumers, costing the company almost $15 million. Ironically, the very incentive system designed to create value destroyed it in the long run. What is valued drives action, and Steven Landsburg says that people respond to incentives while the rest is commentary. Amen.

Assumption III: The Creation of Knowledge and Its Appropriate Use Leads to Value Creation

One of the imperatives of the global economy is that individuals and the organizations they belong to must be lifelong learners. They must continue to acquire, create, and use knowledge if they and their organizations are to grow and thrive in our constantly changing and highly competitive world. As Americans, we are uniquely privileged to live in a society that has always valued the creation of knowledge, which continues to produce a constant stream of new products and ideas, and which is still the envy of most of the rest of the world in this respect. The roots of the creative process in our nation undoubtedly have their origins in our history as a pioneering nation, breaking away from a paternalistic colonial beginning, valuing independence and the rights of the individual, and constantly searching for new horizons to explore and conquer.

Entrepreneurs and the market economies in which they prosper thrive because entrepreneurs create *knowledge* that leads to the creation of new goods and services. Most entrepreneurial firms are characterized by creativity and openness, with the owners operating in a team environment along with their employees. Such an atmosphere leads to the production of intellectual as well as physical capital.

The command economies, without exception, were dominated by stultifying conformity, intimidation, and the denial of the entrepreneurial spirit. Thus, the uniform poverty they created in country after country is hardly surprising.

The similarity between command economies and authoritarian, bureaucratic businesses is obvious. Authoritarian organizations not only fail to generate knowledge, they simply *waste* it because their hierarchical structures stymie free expression and encourage mind-wasting conformity. Dozens of books on organizational and societal conformity—some of them classics like William Whyte's *The Organization Man*—have remarked on this phenomenon.[8] Woe is due the organization that wastes its intellectual capital and its human assets because of authoritarian or abusive management practices.

Rensis Likert, the father of contemporary participative and team-based management practices that will be an organizational hallmark of the new millennium, discovered all this nearly four decades ago in his pioneering studies of the power of participation and empowerment (although that term had yet to be developed) to create value. His research showed that companies that practice participative, or what Likert called "System 4," management, consistently outperform firms that are less participative and more authoritarian, or what he called "System 1."[9] His research demonstrates again and again that the more participative firms are superior, especially when *time* is factored in as a variable.[10] In the long run, authoritarian managers and organizations tend to get into trouble, although in the short run they may do well.

The mindset and value set that underlies and facilitates knowledge creation in organizations that create value, is a mindset of genuine *open-mindedness*, which leads to free and open communications in the organization, an atmosphere free of fear and full of trust, and an organizational environment that encourages what Peter Senge calls dialogue as opposed to *discussion*. As we noted in the previous chapter, Senge, writing in *The Fifth Discipline*, uses *discussion* in a rather special way.

> The word *discussion* has the same root as percussion and concussion. It suggests something like a Ping-Pong game where we are hitting the ball back and forth between us. In such a game, the subject of common interest may be analyzed and dissected from many points of view provided by those who take part. Clearly, this can be useful. Yet the purpose of a game is normally *to win*, and in this case, winning means to have one's views accepted by the group. You might occasionally accept part of another person's view to strengthen your own, but you fundamentally want your view to prevail. A sustained emphasis on winning is not compatible, however, with giving priority to coherence and truth. Bohm (Authors' note: David Bohm in *The Special Theory of Relativity*)[11] suggests that what is needed to cause such a change of priorities is *dialogue*, which is a different mode of communication.
>
> By contrast with discussion, the word *dialogue* comes from the Greek dialogos. "Dia" meaning through, "logos" meaning the word, or more broadly, the meaning. Bohm suggests that the original meaning of dialogue was "the meaning of passing on or moving through . . . a free-flow of meaning between people in the sense of a stream that flows between two banks." In dialogue, Bohm contends, a group accesses a larger "pool of common meaning," which cannot be accessed individually. "The whole organizes the parts," rather than trying to pull the parts into a whole. The purpose

of dialogue is to go beyond any one individual's understanding. "We are not trying to win in dialogue. We all win if we are doing it right." People are no longer primarily in opposition, nor can they be said to be interacting, rather they are participating in this pool of common meaning, which is capable of constant development and change.[12]

Senge's (and Bohm's) analysis of what constitutes true dialogue is a perfect metaphor for the creation of knowledge, and of value. Today, in many traditional organizational settings, we all too often experience duels of egos, with a great deal of discussion, virtually no dialogue, and the most determined or eloquent speaker winning the day, although the underlying mindsets and file folders of the participants emerged unchanged. In most of these discussions, the people involved do not really listen to each other, since the purpose of the discussion is not the creation of new knowledge, but a value-destroying "win-lose" form of psychological combat. In today's managerial world, where knowledge and creativity are not only power, but king, and where every organizational asset must be exploited fully in order to create value, the importance of creating knowledge through dialogue is greater than ever.

In Value Driven Management, a major purpose of the organization's existence is precisely the creation of knowledge through dialogue, open communications, and good listening, followed by the appropriate use of that knowledge to create value for the firm over the long haul.

Assumption IV: Value Is Subjective

We have noted several times that we love to quantify just about everything, and we are sometimes suspicious of things in life that are inherently subjective (nonquantitative), even though some of the most important things in this earthly passage can never be neatly reduced to numbers. Even the simplest monetary transaction in our society raises surprisingly complex questions of subjectivity. For example, if we were to sell you a cup of coffee for

$1.50, and if you agreed to buy it at that price, it is clearly logical that we value the $1.50 more than the coffee we are selling you, and that *you* value the coffee more than the $1.50 because you are willing to part with it to buy the coffee. Each of the parties has received value in the transaction, but there is a highly subjective zone of values that goes beyond the exchange of the $1.50.

For example, if it is a cold night at the ball park, and you are getting a chill while watching your favorite players' batting averages bounce up and down, you might be willing to spend more than you usually would for a hot cup of coffee, especially if there are no other alternatives in sight. The fact that you are cold has increased the value of the coffee in your mind to more than $1.50, and if we were aware of your actual physical condition we might in fact be able to charge you $2.00 or more. Even in such a simple transactional example, there are other variables that influence the *zone of values* involved in the sale of the coffee.

Economic and noneconomic values often compete and conflict in decision-making situations, and in ways that are engagingly complex and subjective. What do you think is the best car? Your answer may be a type and color that is not appealing to others. The reason why there are so many sizes, shapes, and colors of autos with a variety of options, is that what each of us values in a car, differs.

It is interesting that for many years we have made systematic attempts to take the subjectivity out of business decisions on the assumption that subjectivity is bad. Organizational policy manuals often represent an elaborate written attempt to avoid subjectivity. Performance appraisal forms make use of elaborate rating scales that are then summed up or averaged to provide a quantified rating of an employee's performance with a superficial veneer of objectivity. Personnel selection decisions are made using similar forms. Employees are encouraged to quantify their performance objectives whenever possible. The examples are too many to enumerate fully in this short volume, but they have a common theme: Subjectivity is not O.K., and as a result, common sense and good judgment have suffered.

Unfortunately, most important business decisions are not only complex, they are highly subjective, involving the interplay of numerous value drivers and requiring good managerial and executive judgment. The training of good managerial judgment, as well as encouraging individual decision makers to take responsibility for the judgements they make, are major goals of Value Driven Management.

Assumption V: There Are Value Adders and Destroyers

It is a fact of organizational life that within every firm there are people, processes, and systems that either add value to the organization, or destroy it. Not surprisingly, an organization's employees are a major source of value creation and destruction: well-educated, highly motivated, competent, and creative employees add value. When we use the term "human assets," we are usually referring to such productive people. On the other hand, fearful, unhappy, misplaced, and nonperforming employees destroy value, and in some cases, can be a primary source of organizational value loss. In Assumption XI we discuss the fact that all employees are employees, and so this precept applies equally to the managers and executives employed by the organization.

Value creators are those positive and proactive people who consistently see the proverbial half-empty glass as half-full, and who see the opportunity in even the most difficult situations to create value. They see opportunity where others see only threats. They accept the fact that obstacles are to be expected, and they deal with them. Value destroyers on the other hand are employees who see the glass as already half-empty, and sure to tip over. A survey of employees at Koch Industries was done by Randy Pohlman, using focus group interviews to discuss the major obstacles to value creation. The results of each focus group were the same. Value destroyers are those employees with a bad attitude. Some of these people were very good technically, but their attitudes were so negative that they were almost certain not to fit into Koch's positive culture. We are reminded of a familiar human-resource saying, "If he didn't have such a bad attitude, he'd make a great employee."

The 1995 bankruptcy of Barings PLC, a British investment bank, is a recent and dramatic case in point. In a *Corporate Cash Flow* editorial, Richard Gamble remarked that "a 28-year-old man who flunked high school math, skipped college and had been fined for exposing himself in a disco, single-handedly took down the venerable British merchant banking house that helped to finance the Louisiana Purchase."[13] The man who did the deed was Nick Leeson, a trader based in the bank's Singapore office, who had spectacular early success in the various trades he made for Barings, but who eventually ran amok. Writing in the *Far Eastern Economic Review,* Mark Clifford analyzed young Leeson in an article aptly entitled "Baring Down."

> Armed with little more than a computer screen and the Barings' name, 28-year-old trader Nick Leeson went on a spending spree and racked up major losses. Regulators around the world are sorting through the wreckage of the disastrous trades that have destroyed the House of Baring, a merchant bank that sometimes appeared more powerful than the governments it financed. Singapore-based Leeson built up massive positions in futures contracts betting that Japanese stock prices would rise. As the market fell instead, Leeson apparently kept doubling and re-doubling his bets. Barings belatedly realized that something was wrong. Losses were estimated at more than $1.2 billion, about triple the bank's capital.[14]

Analysts have subsequently suggested that Barings' downfall was due to lack of controls and to "sloppy supervision."[15] Nick Leeson's punishment for his disastrous trades was a jail term to be served in Singapore, while Barings' cross to bear (pun intended) was its total bankruptcy. The case is memorable and melodramatic, but it is a powerful illustration of how one highly placed employee can effectively—if inadvertently—not only destroy value, but also destroy an entire company.

While de-motivated employees with an "attitude" (which we can translate quite literally as a bad attitude) may be a major cause of organizational problems, our experience as management consultants has taught us another important lesson: Poor management systems routinely lead to poor performance and to the destruction of value over time. Total quality management

(TQM), as developed by Dr. W. Edwards Deming,[16] has fallen from favor in American industry in the late 1990s, but Deming's insights (and his fourteen principles of TQM) are no flavor-of-the-month management fad. One of the philosophical bases of TQM, in fact, is its emphasis on the continuous improvement of management systems and core work processes, and its recognition of the fact that quality is a precondition for competing in the global economy.

> Unlike some of the management fads that took hold in American industry in previous generations . . . the TQM movement did not promise yet another quick fix for industry's problems. Indeed, its philosophy of continuous improvement was a sobering reminder to management and workers alike that a commitment to quality was going to be both long-term and continuing. Even though literally millions of words have been written about the history and practice of TQM, its impact on the workplace and on management practices and skills has not always been fully understood.[17]

Companies that have used TQM, and used it well—thousands have not—have discovered that its effective use requires a virtual transformation of the workplace: The TQM movement has caused companies to become more focused on improving the management and systems of companies rather than assuming that most problems are caused by poor performance by nonmanagement employees. Dr. Deming's admonition to "stop evaluating employees and start leading them," resulted in many organizations listening more to their nonmanagement employees, getting their participation, empowering them, and developing more powerful value-creating systems.

Assumption VI: Markets Provide Vital Information

Some 200 years ago, the English economist Adam Smith observed that there is an "invisible hand" present in market economies that guides their operation, including such vitally important tasks as the setting of prices through the interaction of supply and demand for goods and services, as well as the allocation of resources.[18] Smith was right, of course, and over the centuries the notion of the invisible hand has become far and away the best known of all economic metaphors or analogies. Each and every day, every free-market economy in the world automatically and effortlessly generates billions and billions of pieces of vital economic information that are important to the lives and welfare of millions of individuals, as well as to organizational decision-makers who hope to create value for their firms.

One of the great failures of centrally-planned, command economies has been the total failure of planners to allocate resources efficiently. For many years factory managers in the old Soviet Union were given annual production quotas, and their creative efforts to achieve these frequently irrational targets have given rise to legendary—and perhaps apocryphal—stories. One such tale has to do with the manager of a factory that produced chandeliers, who was given his annual quota in pounds. Later, after dozens of chandeliers in Soviet buildings began tearing loose from ceilings and plunging right on down through floors, investigators discovered that the aerodynamic fixtures had been cleverly filled with concrete or lead. The factory manager had achieved his quota, but at the expense of destroying value—and buildings![19]

In market economies, of course, resources flow to those organizations that are the most productive and profitable—to those that create value over time. Logically, such a flow of resources should lead to the creation of even more value in the long run, since the best organizations are run by the most creative and productive people. A further logical implication of such resource flow is that free-market economies should create more value over time, including prosperity and creative self-actualization, than centrally planned ones. One of the sad legacies of communism in Eastern Europe has been the systematic sapping of creativity and enthusiasm among workers, a psychological legacy that continues to plague such countries as the reunited Germany. Workers, in what was formerly East Germany, have still not matched their West German counterparts in efficiency nearly a decade after reunion. According to Professor Lothar Hoehne (who escaped from

East Germany several decades ago on his second attempt, after being captured and jailed on his first, and then fled to the United States to do a Ph.D. in International Economics at the University of Wisconsin), it will be another generation or two before German workers in the East will fully recover from the effects of four decades of communism.[20]

While the invisible hand of the market automatically allocates resources within the economy, and *to* organizations, the lack of a market structure *within* organizations often present decision makers with major difficulties in allocating resources internally. When Randy Pohlman was working at Koch Industries, the company launched a major effort to develop internal markets within the organization, in keeping with the principles of what long-time CEO Charles Koch has come to call *market-based management*.[21] Firms such as Koch, Amoco, Xerox and many others have realized the value that can be created by the use of market information within the organization. To begin achieving these types of internal markets, support groups such as human resources, accounting, finance, and marketing sell their services to the operating units. The creation of such a process is startling, and a revelation to the people involved: Market-based prices begin to convey the real costs of doing business, and the information thus developed can lead to fundamental changes in how internal decisions are made.

For example, prior to the introduction of internal markets at Koch, the company was considering the purchase of an additional corporate jet, since the existing fleet was being heavily used. After a market price was established for the use of the aircraft, however, Koch suddenly had one corporate jet too many. The jets had previously been a free good, but now they had become a cost of doing business. When people have information about costs and must pay for internal services, and are held accountable for their results, accountability takes on a whole new dimension.

Unfortunately, internal market structures cannot be created effortlessly and automatically. Transaction cost issues are a problem. Employee morale sometimes drops during the implementation process and this type of change can be very threatening. Initially, the profit focus may change from value creation for the entire organization to unit- or department-centered profitability. Despite these problems, however, companies that make systematic and sustained use of internal markets and avoid the flavor-of-the-month syndrome, discover the liberating power of free enterprise within the organization, as William Halal, Ali Geranmayeh, and John Pourdehnad point out in their groundbreaking 1993 book, *Internal Markets: Bringing the Power of Free Enterprise Inside Your Organization.*[22]

Assumption VII: Opportunity Costs Affect Value

Almost every decision we make, and every major decision, involves significant *opportunity costs*. When we pursue one opportunity, we must forsake others: Our opportunity cost is the cost of foregone opportunities. The Nova Southeastern MBA students incur opportunity costs when they enter the weekend MBA program because they must forsake other activities for an eighteen-month period.

While understanding the concept of opportunity costs is really quite simple, it is surprising how often the concept is not applied in the real world, where its use can create value for any organization wishing to take advantage of the related principle of *comparative advantage.* Take, for example, the decision a company CEO made to invest $50,000 a year in a new administrative assistant. His father-in-law, the Chairman of the Board who inherited the company from *his* father-in-law, calls our CEO to denounce him for this "wasteful" decision in view of the austerity program that the firm has just launched. "How could you be so extravagant?" he demands angrily. "Dad, you just don't understand opportunity costs and comparative advantage," our hero responds brightly. "This decision is going to create value for our firm. Let me explain it to you."

Hiring a *competent* administrative assistant will free up 15 to 20 hours a week of the CEO's time to do things where the CEO has a comparative advantage, such as engaging in strategic planning or analyzing new growth opportunities. The administrative assistant's comparative advantage is in doing vital but time-consuming administrative duties. The net result of a decision based on opportunity costs and comparative advantage will be increased productivity and the creation of value for the firm—things that even the somewhat benighted Chairman of the Board can be expected to comprehend.

Would it be wise for the world's finest brain surgeon, who is also the world's finest cleaner of brain-surgery operating rooms, to do both jobs: the surgery, and the clean-up? We can hear our readers chorusing in unison: "A no-brainer." And right you are. The surgeon's comparative advantage is in saving lives by performing brain surgery. Someone else can be hired who is fully capable of cleaning up the operating theater, even though this person cannot perform surgery. Using the surgeon's unique talents to the fullest extent clearly creates value, in a wonderful way—and lives are saved that would otherwise be lost.

Assumption VIII: Order Is Spontaneous

When ambitious authors like us set out to write a book, we sit down and develop a detailed chapter-by-chapter plan for the forthcoming volume. We can assure you that this is a labor intensive and deadly serious activity that routinely leads to the most spirited dialogues. After much agonizing, when the plan has been finalized, we set out to actually write the book. Our readers can guess what happens then. We make numerous changes in the original outline, adding many topics and case examples, and deleting many others. Chapters are subject to complex permutations and combinations. More dialogues occur. And when the book is finally finished, it bears some relation to the original plan, but not entirely. Yet it is a good product that has in many ways evolved as it was being written. It has organized itself! The book has been finished, and more or less on time, because we finally had the wisdom to recognize the universal principle that *order is spontaneous.*

The notion that market economies spontaneously bring order to economic expansion and development that is superficially chaotic, is the most fundamental insight of the late Nobel laureate in economics, Friedrich von Hayek, who died in 1992. Hayek deeply believed in the profound ability of market economies to generate order without design, and without the attempts of central planners, strategic planners, and hierarchies of every description to plan and control economic change. Management guru Tom Peters is an unabashed admirer of Hayek. Writing in 1996 in *Forbes* magazine, Peters agrees with Hayek's contention that the workings (and outcomes) of market economies are inherently unknowable.

> And Hayek's lifelong intellectual pursuit grew out of this idea: that the dense, decentralized economic/trading network that emerged millenniums ago quickly became unknowable. Moreover, the chief vehicle that moves economics and civilizations forward is unplanned experimentation, per se, among billions of individuals who do not know one another. Along the way, successful experiments are emulated. (Very few experiments succeed immediately for what we call the "right" reasons—i.e., "according to plan." The rest emerge, often over a long period of time, for the "wrong" reasons— i.e., unplanned, unimagined, mostly unimaginable.) Unsuccessful experiments, the vast majority, simply drop by the wayside. Thus the process of economic expansion is humbling, irrational and—by definition—not amenable to central planning and control. "Order generated without design," Hayek wrote, "can far outstrip plans men consciously contrive."[23]

Hayek's work deals with entire societies and economies and not with business organizations (or authors), who *should* do planning, but with some caveats. Writing on this topic in a recent book, *The Rise and Fall of Strategic Planning*, Henry Mintzberg reaches the conclusion that strategic analysis and the formulation of plans are not futile or worthless, but neither are they the cure-all for every business problem that they are sometimes claimed to be.[24] Organizational vision, and the strategies and plans needed to realize it, must be flexible if it is to be successful, Mintzberg argues. This reminds your authors, naturally enough, of the plan that was originally developed for this book.

A clear implication of Hayek's thinking is that organizational decision makers who develop the mindset that order is spontane-ous, and who thus develop strategies and plans that are nimble and flexible, will consistently create more value for their firms than will planners who commit their companies to rigid long-term budgets or strategic plans. File-folderitis, complicated by hardening of the categories, is not adaptive behavior in dealing with the vagaries of market economies, or when one is faced by the challenge of writing a book on Value Driven Management.

Assumption IX: Values Can Compete or Be Complementary

We have remarked earlier that there are times when personal and organizational values will be congruent, and times when they will be in conflict with one another, or be incongruent. Often it is economic values—the need to have an adequate income, and the "perks" that go with high income levels—that conflict with other important values, as we noted in discussing the Allport-Vernon-Lindzey *Study of Values* in Chapter 2. For example, we have all faced the dilemma of whether we should be good, loyal organizational types, and spend long, long hours at work, or whether we should be good, loyal family types, and spend more hours than we customarily do with our spouses and children. We often think of such value clashes in "either-or" or "win-lose" terms: If we work more hours, we will earn more money, but enjoy less precious time with our families. It seems to be a zero-sum game. What our customers, suppliers, employers, owners, third parties, competitors, and society value are often in conflict. The value conflict is one of the great challenges of running any organization successfully. A constantly shifting optimal balance is the key to success.

In a recent article in *Harvard Business Review* entitled "Work and Life: The End of the Zero-Sum Game," authors Stewart Friedman, Perry Christensen, and Jessica DeGroot observe that the traditional assumption that work and personal values are competing priorities—or dichotomous—is being challenged by a small but growing number of managers who are treating the work-life question as complementary, and who are creating value by adopting a win-win philosophy.[25] Many such managers are "flying under the radar of officially sanctioned programs," but they appear to be right: "In the cases we have studied, the new approach has yielded tangible payoffs for organizations and individual employees."[26]

According to Friedman, Christensen, and DeGroot, such managers are guided by three interactive and "mutually reinforcing" principles: (1) they clarify what is important, including their business priorities as well as the personal needs and priorities of their employees; (2) they recognize and support their employees as whole people, acknowledging that they have roles outside the office and the organization; and (3) they continually experiment with the way work is done, and look for approaches that enhance organizational performance while also facilitating employees' personal pursuits. This three-pronged approach leads to a "virtuous cycle," where trust, commitment, energy, and loyalty are mutually reinforced.

The article presents numerous case studies that demonstrate the power and value of the author's approach: the *leveraged* approach. It lies at the end of a continuum containing three distinct types, beginning with the *trade-off* approach where either the business or personal life wins, but not both; continuing on to the *integrated* approach, where employee and manager work together to satisfy both sets of needs (a practice increasingly prevalent in a full-employment economy where firms need to keep talented people); and going on to the far end of the continuum, the *leveraged* approach where the three principles are unified.

> Taken together, the three principles fall at the far end of the continuum—the *leveraged* approach, in which the practices used to strike a work-life balance actually add value to the business. Not only do the three principles seem to help people live more satisfying personal lives, but they also help identify inefficiencies in work processes and illuminate better ways to get work done.[27]

The leveraged approach not only creates value for organizations, managers, and employees alike, but it requires that managers get away from the traditional mindset that "face time"—the amount of time employees put in physically—is more important than productivity, one of the keys to creating organizational value. The article is a "must read" for any student of Value Driven Management, and illustrates the need to harmonize and integrate values in the process of creating value.

Value Driven Management approaches the important topic of business ethics from the same point of view. As employees, managers, and executives of business organizations (although in the context of Value Driven Management we are all employees), we are frequently faced with tough choices in the world of work. In many such situations, our personal values come into conflict with organizational values, and there may be powerful organizational pressures upon us to make choices that conflict sharply with personal values such as fairness and honesty. As Gary Gardiner and O. C. Ferrell point out in *In Pursuit of Ethics: Tough Choices in the World of Work*, the research of Dr. Stanley Milgram at Yale University in the 1960s and 1970s (described in detail in his 1974 book, *Obedience to Authority*) showed that a truly shocking percentage of a group of ordinary, working Americans will obey the commands of an authority figure dressed in a white lab coat (Dr. Milgram himself) to administer electric shocks to an innocent person that they thought might be fatal.[28] Despite their unanimous conviction that they were doing wrong, 26 members of a group of 40 subjects in one of Milgram's early experiments administered fatal "shocks" (the shock generator was in fact a dummy) after being given verbal commands to do so by Milgram, and without being threatened in any way. The issue of power in organizations, and its use and abuse in creating or destroying value is so important, we believe, that we will return to this topic in the final chapters of this book.

Assumption X: Any Action May Have Unintended Consequences

The American people have embraced technology, have made excellent use of it in their personal and professional lives, and still lead the world in the development of new technologies. Our long-time love affair with technology sometimes has a serious drawback, however, as Edward Tenner (former editor of the *Princeton University Press*) pointed out in a 1996 book, *Why Things Bite Back: Technology and the Revenge of Unintended Consequences*: New technology sometimes has negative and totally unintended consequences, and it has a nasty tendency to bite back.[29]

The book is full of dozens of examples of new technology's "revenge effects," the totally unanticipated and sometimes disastrous consequences of a technological fix for a problem. The name "Titanic" is now synonymous with disaster, but when that magnificent vessel was built, it was designed to be the safest ship in the world, and virtually unsinkable. Convinced of its invulnerability, the captain and crew took risks on its maiden voyage that they should have never considered, and the rest, of course, is history. Superhard football helmets that were designed for the wearer's protection have inadvertently resulted in serious injuries to other players struck by them. Our highly touted flood control and levee systems, the pride of the Army Corps of Engineers, encouraged development on flood plains that were supposedly safe, but which were in fact highly vulnerable to floods inadvertently worsened by the systems, resulting in rivers like the Mississippi being turned into giant ditches during major floods such as the 1993 disaster in the Midwest.

While Tenner's book is fascinating reading, we need not belabor you with every example in it; instead let us cut directly to the chase: What can we do to reduce the revenge effects of new technology? Tenner's prescription is highly commonsensical in that he simply recommends that when we are evaluating new technologies, we should take more time to think things through—to make a sober and careful assessment of the technology's promise and its limitations. Sophisticated computer technology and the rise of the Internet have had a major effect on both management and the workplace, and given rise to a whole new type of commerce, but the net effect of computer technology on mankind has yet to be computed. Internet commerce, for example, has led to unexpected new types of consumer fraud, and the accompanying development of vast databases has generated unprecedented invasion of privacy issues. The development of ultra-sophisticated corporate and military computer systems has led to the rise of a generation of computer hackers who take devilish delight in subverting such systems, at great cost to their developers. An assessment process for new technology such as Tenner recommends will surely result in more frequent creation of value, and fewer unintended consequences of promising new technological developments.

Organizational decision makers should undoubtedly pay attention to the same principle before taking action. Had Sears' executives taken more time to think things through before they launched their auto-repair incentive scheme, for example, they could have saved the company a bundle. In the field of human resource management, bungled terminations—as we have already noted in Chapter 2—often come back to haunt employers because the termination process has not been carefully thought through, and careful and adequate disciplinary steps, including documentation, have not been taken, and angry ex-employees may either file expensive lawsuits or commit acts of violence against their former employers.[30] Such unintended consequences can wreak havoc, of course, with an organization's attempts to create value. Careful and complex thought using rigorous analytical processes and methods, and the exercise of diligence in considering decisions or actions, are of vital importance to almost every organization. In all important decisions and actions, the possibility of serious unintended consequences must be carefully considered. The old bromide, "Look before you leap," is an irresistible editorial comment here.

Decision makers often fail to think things through when they are under a high degree of stress. Years ago Princeton University psychologists Harold Schroder, Michael Driver, and Sigmund Streufert reported research in a 1967 volume, *Human Information Processing*, that shows that when people are dealing with maladaptively high levels of stress, their thinking becomes much more concrete and "black-white": They process much less information in decision-making situations, consider fewer alternatives, and generally are much less likely to think things through.[31] This research also demonstrated, however, that when people are carefully trained to use complex information-processing techniques, they withstand the negative effects of stress much better, and the quality of their decision making holds up much more strongly than for persons who have not had such training. Individual and organizational training in the complex analytic-thinking process lies at the very heart of Value Driven Management, is vital to its implementation, and is a continuing theme in this book.

Assumption XI: All Employees Are Employees

We believe that in an organization that is truly committed to maximizing value over time, *all members* of the organization must be responsible for creating value; and from this point of view, all of them are employees—even though they may have different job titles and different responsibilities. Quite literally, every person working for an organization is an employee, from the CEO to the night watchperson, but the traditional and hierarchical mindset or file-folder about organizations is that some of us are managers or executives and a lot of us are employees.

In the team-oriented and participative forms of organization that are now emerging, where formal hierarchy is emphasized less, and collegial cooperation emphasized more, historical distinctions between management and labor—the oldest dichotomy in the workplace, heavy with the burden of hundreds of years of negative connotations—are beginning to diminish. This is not to imply, however, that we are all now equal in terms of the magnitude of our rights to make decisions in the organization. It is to suggest that each of us has the responsibility to seek out opportunities where we can create the greatest value for our organization, to exploit to the fullest any comparative advantages that we bring to our firm as one of its responsible and productive employees.

Each employee must take personal responsibility for the development of the skills and abilities they need to lead and manage their work lives. On the other hand, the top leaders in the organization must realize the tremendous impact it will have if each employee reaches their full potential in the workplace. Too often, top management fails to ensure that all employees are able to share the vision of the organization, understand their place in it, and have the skills and abilities to contribute to it. If an organization implements Value Driven Management, it should make sure all employees—at every level—understand it and how it is used.

Eleven Value-Creating Assumptions, Best Management Practices, and Organizational Synergy

The assumptions that underlie the philosophy of Value Driven Management are not only practical, philosophical, psychological, economic, and organizational statements that have "stand alone" value; they are also statements that are intertwined, that overlap, that harmonize, that lead us in new directions, and that create value in and of themselves. Again and again, they suggest to us what the best management practices are, both current and emerging, that will facilitate the development and implementation of Value Driven Management in organizations. Taken in total, they point to a management philosophy and set of tools that will enhance creativity, improve productivity, and maximize the creation of value over time in organizations that adopt the philosophy and use the tools wisely

Case 4-1

Consolidated Diesel Company and the Creation of Value

Consolidated Diesel Company plant in Whitakers, North Carolina, is a textbook case in the creation of value—value that has been created and sustained over a 20-year period through a continuing focus on internal cultural values and individual employee values. The plant is hardly romantic: It is 1.2 million feet square, it churns out about 650 diesel engines a day, and it has a traditional assembly line. But there is something very different about this plant, especially when it is compared to many traditional manufacturing operations. Says Curtis Sittenfeld, writing in *Fast Company*, "There is nothing novel about the plant's assembly line. There is nothing sexy about its product. But inside this factory, something revolutionary is going on."[32]

According to Sittenfeld, the plant is uniquely productive because its employees are part of an ongoing social experiment in granting employees a uniquely extraordinary level of responsibility, thus the title of his *Fast Company* article, "Powered by the People."[33] The plant turns out an engine every 72 seconds that the assembly line is operational (most of them are used in tractors, trucks and similar vehicles), the turnover rate is less than 2 percent, the plant has never had a significant layoff, and it has one supervisor for every 100 employees (compared to the industry average of about one for every 25 employees). Sittenfeld notes that the low supervisor-to-employee ratio yields savings of about $1 million a year, and further savings are generated by an injury rate that is about one-fifth of the national average.

Consolidated Diesel was formed as a joint venture between Cummins Engine Co. and J. I. Case Corp. in 1980, and ever since its opening, the plant has made use of a team-based management system, an approach based on early research in British coal mines that showed—not surprisingly—that workers are more satisfied and more productive when they have a say in determining how they work. Consolidated Diesel has developed policies and practices in four key areas, according to Sittenfeld, that have made the system work. First, the company plays fair: Every worker gets a bonus, or no one does, for example, and entire teams are switched from day to night shifts every two weeks. Second, the plant makes use of extensive cross training, where workers may be doing quality inspections one day, but working on a machine the next.

Third, the company involves employees in designing solutions to plant problems. In 1998, customer demand was so high that the teams designed new schedules to allow for more flexibility among the shifts. Fourth, the teams have *real* responsibility, including hiring—and sometimes firing—their own members. Consolidated Diesel has high expectations for employees, and rewards them commensurately. Aside from bonuses, highly productive employees are also often rewarded with promotions. Sittenfeld quotes the plant's director of human resources with regard to expectations.

> ''Expectations in a team environment are much higher here than at any other place where I've worked,'' says Larry Williams, 42, director of human resources. ''And a lot of those expectations are ones that we place on ourselves. Being part of a team creates a different sense of accountability. Everybody expects more from everybody else.''[34]

Williams also notes that 90 percent of the employees call him by his first name, which is unusual in the respectful American South. When the plant first opened, shiftwide state-of-the-plant meetings were held every quarter, but the sheer size of these meetings—with as many as 700 employees in attendance—defeated their purpose.

Jim Lyons, the general manager, solved the large-meeting problem by dividing the employees into 15 groups, which now meet separately over a two-day period. The number of questions asked by workers has quadrupled as the result of this change. ''We share the good, the bad, and the ugly,'' Sittenfeld quotes Lyons as saying.[35] The company also has an in-house weekly newsletter, and a closed-circuit TV network to facilitate communications. Lyons is quoted again in closing Sittenfeld's *Fast Company* piece: "When good people are given good information, they typically make good decisions."[36]

Questions for Discussion and Reflection

1. Why are more plants not operated in the way that Consolidated Diesel manages its Whitakers plant?

2. Is the plant's high level of productivity and profitability likely to continue?

3. What are the critical factors in the success of the plant?

4. Are the values and expectations of the teams of workers in the plant congruent with those of management?

Endnotes

1. Abraham H. Maslow, *Motivation and Personality* (New York: Harper, 1954).

2. Ibid.

3. Ludwig von Mises, *Human Action: A Treatise on Economics* (New Haven: Yale University Press, 1963).

4. Ibid., 12.

5. Ibid., 13.

6. Steven E. Landsburg, *The Armchair Economist* (New York: Free Press, 1993), 3.

7. Gareth R. Jones, Jennifer M. George, and Charles W. L. Hill, *Contemporary Management* (New York: Irwin/McGraw-Hill, 1998), 280.

8. William H. Whyte, Jr., *The Organization Man* (New York: Simon & Schuster, 1972).

9. Rensis Likert, *New Patterns of Management* (New York: McGraw-Hill, 1961).

10. Rensis Likert, *The Human Organization* (New York: McGraw-Hill, 1967).

11. David Bohm, *The Special Theory of Relativity* (New York: W. A. Benjamin, 1965).

12. Peter Senge, *The Fifth Discipline* (New York: Doubleday Currency, 1994), 240.

13. Richard H. Gamble, "Give Stars to the Young Guns," *Corporate Cash Flow*, April 1995, 2.

14. Mark Clifford, "Baring Down," *Far Eastern Economic Review*, 9 March 1995, 61.
15. Ibid.
16. W. Edwards Deming, *Out of the Crisis* (Boston: MIT Press, 1986).
17. Gareth S. Gardiner, *21st Century Manager* (Princeton, NJ: Peterson's/Pacesetter Books, 1996), 21–22.
18. Adam Smith, *An Inquiry into the Nature and Causes of the Wealth of Nations* (Edinburgh: A. and C. Black, 1862).
19. Some such stories may be apocryphal, but the inefficient distribution of resources that routinely occurs in centrally-planned economies is definitely not fictional.
20. Dr. Lothar Hoehne now teaches courses in International Economics in the Wayne Huizenga Graduate School of Business and Entrepreneurship at Nova Southeastern University.
21. Wayne Gable and Jerry Ellig, *Introduction to a Market-based Management* (Fairfax, VA: Center for Market Processes, 1993).
22. William E. Halal, Ali Geranmayeh, and John Pourdehnad, *Internal Markets: Bringing the Power of Free Enterprise Inside Your Organization* (New York: John Wiley & Sons, 1993).
23. Tom Peters, "Let Chaos Reign," *Forbes*, 26 August 1996, 112–113.
24. Henry Mintzberg, *The Rise and Fall of Strategic Planning* (New York: Prentice Hall, 1994).
25. Stewart D. Friedman, Perry Christensen, and Jessica DeGroot, "Work and Life: The End of the Zero-Sum Game," *Harvard Business Review*, November-December 1998, 119–129.
26. Ibid., 120.
27. Ibid., 129.
28. O. C. Ferrell and Gareth S. Gardiner, *In Pursuit of Ethics* (Springfield, IL: Smith Collins, 1991), 14–15.
29. Edward Tenner, *Why Things Bite Back: Technology and the Revenge of Unintended Consequences* (New York: Knopf, 1996).
30. Gareth S. Gardiner, *Tough-Minded Management* (New York: Fawcett Columbine, 1993).
31. Harold M. Schroder, Michael Driver, and Sigmund Streufert, *Human Information Processing* (New York: Holt, Rinehart, and Winston, 1967).
32. Curtis Sittenfeld, "Powered by the People," *Fast Company*, July-August 1999, 181.
33. Ibid., 179–188.
34. Ibid., 186.
35. Ibid., 187.
36. Ibid.

Part II

Value Drivers in Action

Chapter 5

The Creation and Destruction of Value Over Time: Cases, Examples, and Anecdotes

We have already noted that value drivers typically do not exist in isolation, but they interact with each other in highly complex ways. Often, the interaction is synergistic: In some cases, a number of value drivers will flow together and create value in an unusual or innovative way. It is sometimes difficult to single out which value drivers are more or less important in a given decision-making situation, but there are also cases and situations where individual values will interact with external and internal culture in a remarkable way, as was the case during the Extra-Strength Tylenol poisoning scare of the 1980s in which value-driven decision makers at Johnson & Johnson made courageous and farsighted decisions that created value, not only for the company, but for American and global consumers as well. Alas, other companies, like Exxon during the *Exxon Valdez* oil spill disaster, made decisions where important value drivers were discounted or ignored, and the resulting decisions were disastrous to everyone in-volved—value was destroyed, and not created. This lengthy section of the book pulls out value drivers for singular scrutiny, and also explores how intricately interrelated they can be in the decision-making process.

Why is it that some companies, like Johnson & Johnson during the Extra-Strength Tylenol poisoning scare of the early 1980s, face a major organizational crisis with coolness and dignity, and take smart, proactive action that can actually turn the problem into a plus for the organization, creating value along the way, while others stumble and fall, as Exxon did after the *Exxon Valdez* spilled millions of gallons of crude oil into the previously pristine waters of Alaska's Prince William Sound in 1989? Why do some organizations react positively to the mistakes that are inevitable in running any major business (and exacerbated by the roles played by competitors and third parties) while others compound their mistakes with cover-ups, denials, or self-defeating stonewalling behavior? There is no single and definitive answer to these questions, but a careful analysis of these organizations, including a clear understanding of their often unique internal cultures, as well as the external cultures they face (or perceive that they face), complicated and compounded by the values of decision makers within these companies and the values of their customers, then made more complex by supplier values and the values of company owners, will reveal the logic of their decision-making processes.

We are simply saying that the complexity of major organizational decisions can best be understood by inspecting the values that have driven them in any one of these major decisions or organizational crises. Value Driven Management assumes that value drivers are normally interwoven and interrelated, but in many of the cases that appear in this section of the book, we find one or two value drivers that seem to have had a disproportionate impact on the situation. We move on, then, to a discussion of value drivers and situations revealing their influence at work.

Value Driver 1: External Cultural Values

``Is Denny's ever going to learn? The restaurant chain is facing another complaint of discriminatory treatment three years after paying $54 million to settle civil rights lawsuits. Now a lawsuit has been filed alleging that some Asian and Asian-American students were unfairly denied service at a Denny's in Syracuse, N.Y., last April and then were attacked by a crowd while the restaurant's security guards stood by.''—*The Los Angeles Times* in a 1997 editorial.

In many decisions within an organization, external cultural values must be taken into account if value is to be maximized. This is clearly the case with external cultural values for *customers*, but this will be dealt with in the section on Value Driver 4. Other external cultural values can have a profound impact upon the value of an organization, but they are not given exclusive consideration when decisions are made or actions are taken. In the examples given in each section, you will see what happens when the effect of the external environment is taken into account in the decision-making process, or when it was not.

On March 24, 1989, in an accident that has become famous, the *Exxon Valdez* ran aground on well-charted Blye Reef as it was leaving Valdez Harbor in Prince William Sound, Alaska, and about eleven million gallons of crude oil spilled out through its ruptured hull into the icy waters. The ship's captain, Joseph Hazelwood, who had a long and well-documented history of alcohol abuse, and who was in command of the huge Exxon tanker that fateful night, was later determined to be drunk in the galley when the ship ran aground. "On the day of the accident, Mr. Hazelwood consumed at least three and possibly up to 14 vodka drinks just hours before the tanker pulled out of the Valdez terminal carrying more than ten million gallons of Alaskan crude . . . Shipmates allegedly saw that the captain was drunk when the ship left port."[1] The environmental damage from the huge spill was frightening: The heavy crude oil affected about 1,300 miles of Alaska coastline to varying degrees; thousands and thousands of birds and marine mammals were covered with oil, and many later died despite intensive clean-up efforts; major stocks of fish were affected; and Prince William Sound and large portions of the Gulf of Alaska became an oily mess. Exxon received bad publicity over the huge spill, if we may engage in a major understatement of the impact of the incident.

The company clearly had very little perception of how powerfully and angrily Americans, and people around the world, would react to the magnitude of the environmental damage caused by the spill. The story drew major media coverage for months, in both print and the electronic media. Every television network ran extensive footage of dead birds and mammals, like the lovable sea otter, with their pitiful bodies covered by thick sludge, and fouled beaches were also featured in the coverage. Alaskan fishermen were interviewed again and again, and spoke eloquently about how the spill had damaged their harvests. The publicity was, in a word, tremendous, and Exxon's handling of the spill outraged the public.

Although the company eventually paid roughly $2.5 billion to clean up the mess, its insensitivity to strong environmental values in American culture cost it even more when an Alaska jury awarded $5 billion in punitive damages against Exxon in 1995. The lawyer who represented the plaintiffs in the case, Brian B. O'Neill, commented in *Business Insurance* that Exxon's arrogance was one of the main reasons for the jury's large judgment, as well as its insensitive corporate culture.

> You wonder, "How do you get such an award?" The answer is Exxon did not know how to treat its fellow man. They have $140 billion in annual revenues, they are the 26th largest company in the world and they do not live in the same world as we do. They failed to realize that honesty and contrition work, while arrogance and disingenuousness do not. Mr. O'Neill said immediately after the accident, "Exxon shot itself in the foot on several fronts." At trial, jurors heard a recording of an onsite Exxon public relations official saying something to the effect of, "I don't care if anyone cleans up any oil, just get some suckers out there so it looks like it." "I doubt the jury was very impressed with that," Mr. O'Neill quipped.[2]

Incredibly, while then Chairman Lawrence Rawl signed a letter of apology that was published in *The Wall Street Journal* and *The New York Times*, he may never have even read it, according to O'Neill, and it is well documented that he never visited the site of the spill.

Exxon may not be the all-time champion among companies that have not been sensitive enough to the values of cultures external to the firm. Denny's restaurant chain has had similar problems. For years the company had been the subject of complaints by African-American customers that they had been denied service at various Denny's restaurants, and in 1994 the chain agreed to pay $46 million to settle a discrimination suit filed by six black Secret Service agents who alleged that they had been denied service at a restaurant in Annapolis, Maryland. One would think that such a hefty settlement (accompanied, naturally, by reams and reams of bad publicity) would constitute a healthy learning experience for this organization; but at least two subsequent incidents involving alleged discrimination led to the question raised by *The Los Angeles Times* in the August 31, 1997, editorial quoted above: "Is Denny's ever going to learn?"

In April 1997 the company again blundered badly when one of its restaurants in Syracuse, New York, refused to serve a group of Asian and Asian-American students, as we noted in the *Times* editorial. The *Times* commented further in the same editorial that:

> The Asians and Asian-Americans, most of them Syracuse University students, said they were waiting for a table when they noticed that other customers, who were white, were seated ahead of them. When they complained, the students said the manager told them to leave and had them escorted outside by two security guards, and one allegedly shoved a student. In the parking lot, the students said, they were assaulted by a group of white customers while the two security guards, both off-duty Onondaga County sheriff's deputies, stood by. Two students were knocked unconscious.[3]

Is it too judgmental to suggest at this point that it was Denny's that had apparently been knocked unconscious in the wake of the prior $46 million settlement? But wait, there is more yet to come.

In 1998, at a Denny's restaurant in Ocoee, Florida, near Disney World, it happened again. Denny's denial of service to a group of black sixth-grade students was covered by the Jacksonville-based *Florida Times Union*:

> Four years after settling a discrimination lawsuit for $46 million, Denny's apologized yesterday to 40 black sixth-

graders and their chaperones who said they were denied service at a Florida restaurant. The group from Baltimore was on a field trip to Disney World Thursday
when they stopped at the Denny's in Ocoee. They said
they were not greeted or seated. After seating themselves, they said they waited 20 minutes before some received menus, and left an hour later without being
served while white customers who entered later were
helped. "We apologize to the students and chaperones
who did not feel welcome during their visit," Denny's
President John A. Romandetti said in a statement. "It is
clear that these customers do not feel they were treated
with the courtesy and respect that we pledge to every
Denny's guest. For that, we are sorry." The complaint
was reported by Denny's to the Office of Civil Rights,
which reports to the Justice Department, Romandetti
said.[4]

Despite its continuing problems in providing acceptable service
to minority customers, the company at least apologized quickly
and publicly for its Florida failure.

Perhaps there is hope for the company, though. Early in 1999
the *Detroit News* reported that Advantica Restaurant Group, Inc.,
the parent company of Denny's and several other chains, was
spending $2 million on a series of Denny's anti-racism commer-
cials. Advantica was also making progress, according to the *News*,
toward achieving some of the minority-inclusion goals it had
agreed in settling the discrimination suits.

To help settle the allegations against Denny's, its parent
company (then known as Flagstar Cos.) entered into an
agreement with the National Association for the Ad-
vancement of Colored People to increase the number of
minority-owned restaurants. It later reached a similar
agreement with the Hispanic Association on Corporate
Responsibility. Now minorities make up 48 percent of
Advantica's workforce and 33 percent of its management. Only one Denny's was owned by a black franchi-
see in 1993 and now 123 are black owned. In 1997, the

NAACP awarded Denny's its annual minority business development award for its efforts to provide broader opportunities for minorities.[5]

Exxon and Denny's were at best very slow and reactive in coping with highly publicized crises that erupted unexpectedly in the normal course of doing business, and cost themselves many millions of dollars in legal fees, fines, and other expenses that they might not have incurred if they had been more sensitive and farsighted.

There is an equally famous case involving a company that handled a major and unexpected crisis in a proactive way that created value for it in the long run. That company, of course, is Johnson & Johnson, and the famous case is the Extra-Strength Tylenol poisoning scare in the early 1980s. The case has appeared in many textbooks, but Richard De George provides a succinct summary of how such a crisis situation developed in the fourth edition of his *Business Ethics* book.

On September 30, 1982, three people in the Chicago area died from cyanide introduced into their Extra-Strength Tylenol capsules. The link between the deaths and the capsules was made with remarkable speed, and authorities notified Johnson & Johnson, the manufacturers of Tylenol. As the number of deaths grew—the final total was seven—the firm faced a crisis and potential disaster. Tylenol, a leading pain-reliever, was Johnson & Johnson's single largest brand, accounting for 7.4 percent of its revenue, and 17 to 18 percent of the corporation's income.[6]

The company was faced with a terribly complex decision process according to De George, and the many other authors who have written about the crisis, since there were so many unknowns and uncertainties involved. Where and when had the capsules been tampered with, the Extra-Strength Tylenol removed and replaced with the lethal cyanide? How many deaths would there be, and in what cities or regions? Would temporarily halting sales be a sufficient measure? What actions might the

Food and Drug Administration eventually take? The one relative certainty in the matter was that Johnson & Johnson would take a major short-term financial hit if it pulled the product off retail pharmacy and grocery shelves, including at least $100 million in lost and uninsured sales, accompanied by a drop in J & J's stock price.

The Wall Street analysts were unanimous in arguing that the company should not pull the product because it would lose market share (at the time, Tylenol in all its forms had a 37 percent market share) and never regain it. So much for the wisdom of the analysts, who typically focus heavily (and perhaps far too heavily) on short-term financial data. The company, however, under the leadership of CEO James Burke, made a decision to recall the product immediately. The company's credo is more than just a piece of paper according to almost anyone who has worked at Johnson & Johnson, and the company's decision was totally consistent with its statement of values. Johnson & Johnson's credo begins with a powerful statement: "We believe that our first responsibility is to the doctors, nurses, and patients, to mothers, and to all others who use our products and services."

Under Burke's strong leadership, the company immediately withdrew Extra-Strength Tylenol from the marketplace. There was no hesitation, no dithering around, no sanctimonious statements, and no ands, ifs, or buts. Johnson & Johnson pulled the product, and history (and the marketplace) has judged it kindly. Says *Business Ethics* author De George:

> The company put the safety of the public first, as the company's credo says it should. The incident has grown into a legend, and the reaction of Johnson & Johnson has become a textbook study in how to respond to a tragedy. Not only was the decision hailed as the proper one from an ethical point of view, but also the company handled the aftermath of the tragedy in a skillful manner. The company was open in supplying the public with information, and within 18 months won back 96 percent of its former market share. It did in fact lose $100 million, and the worth of its stock did fall.[7]

Another often-mentioned and value-creating outcome of the poisoning scare was the development of a whole new generation of tamper-proof containers, designed to protect consumers from homicidal maniacs bent on creating mayhem (the perpetrator or perpetrators of the cyanide poisonings have never been caught), and such containers are in widespread use today, as almost every consumer knows.

In a 1987 interview in *New Management* that has since become a classic, William May (at that time director of the program in Business Ethics at the University of Southern California) posed a question that virtually every business organization has to answer at one time or another: Should a business go beyond minimal legal requirements when an ethical issue is involved?[8] Most authors in the field of business ethics, including Gary Gardiner, like to point out that the law usually specifies or defines the minimal moral requirement in a situation, while most ethical theories and formulations call for a higher standard of behavior. Professor May's answer to his own question is a strong "yes," and in his interview with *New Management* entitled, "Good Ethics Is Good Business," he uses Johnson & Johnson's handling of the Extra-Strength Tylenol crisis as a case in point. May repeats the wisdom of the Wall Street analysts: "The financial wizards on Wall Street advised J & J not to recall Tylenol. They thought they'd lose market share."[9] The reaction of the American public to Johnson & Johnson's courageous and value-driven decision, however, may well have been a demonstration of a higher wisdom: woe to the organization that loses sight of the importance of values—like consumer safety—that are an integral part of the external culture, and more power to the organization (like Johnson & Johnson) that recognizes and cherishes those values, and also pays attention to the wishes and desires of its customers.

The examples in this section make it clear that the impact of organizational decisions on the external culture can have a serious impact on value over time. In the cases of Exxon and Denny's, a great deal of value was destroyed that could have rather easily been avoided if different decisions about people and procedures had been made. In both these cases, the values of the external culture were critical to the maximization of value over time. In the case of Johnson & Johnson, appropriate and intelligent decisions and actions were positively received by the external culture, and as a result, value was actually created after a terrible event that could have been catastrophic to the firm.

Value Driver 2: Organizational Cultural Values

"For Koch Industries—and, I believe, for most businesses— constant rethinking and improvement are now more impor- tant than ever. The entire business world faces a revolution that will redefine the role of managers, companies, and entire industries. Development of new technology and changes in consumer desires have always meant change for corpora- tions, but the change occurring today is more fundamental, more rapid, and potentially more devastating than at any time since the industrial revolution."—Charles Koch, CEO, Koch Industries, writing in *Introduction to Market-Based Man- agement.*

Decisions made or actions taken that run counter to the in- ternal culture of an organization may, depending upon their magnitude, seriously decrease value over time unless, of course, they are designed to turn a poor organizational culture into a value-creating one. As you will see in the pages that follow, effec- tive organizational leaders create their own internal culture of value creation. Each organization has its own unique culture, and decisions are made and actions are taken within that cultural context. Employees must take into account how a decision about to be made, or an action about to be taken, will be considered within the organization's culture; as well as the resulting impact on value over time for the organization. Each action taken or decision made should be compared by all employees involved in the decision-making process to what is culturally expected.

Many who marvel at the success of Koch Industries fail to understand the critical importance of its culture to its success. Koch Industries has been described by several commentators, including Lou Dobbs (formerly of CNN's *Management* program), as "The biggest company you have never heard of."[10] The Wich- ita, Kansas-based oil and gas distribution giant is the second largest, privately held company in the country (behind agricul- tural giant Cargill), with 1999 revenues of about $30 billion, and approximately 17,000 employees. Under the strong leadership of longtime CEO Charles Koch, who took over the company in 1967 after his father's death (when it had annual revenues of approximately $200 million, and about 700 employees), the company has grown steadily and remains highly profitable. Koch is a national leader, with oil and gas distribution being its primary business.

For five years, Randy Pohlman was a senior executive at Koch, and during that time he became very familiar with, and helped refine, the concept of market-based management as it was created by Charles Koch and his colleagues at Koch Industries. Market-based management is the process of applying market-based principles and techniques to the management of a business. Koch's CEO remarked:

Our experience has shown that market-based management is a framework within which we can analyze, and even improve upon, other management concepts such as Total Quality Management and Re-engineering. By testing these ideas and programs against the principles of market-based management, we are better able to discern which parts truly add value, and then apply them in a manner that is consistent and complementary with our other ongoing efforts. This helps avoid the "false start" and "flavor of the month" problems that have plagued so many other companies and management approaches. For Koch Industries—and, I believe, for most businesses—constant rethinking and improvement are now more important than ever.[11]

The purpose of developing a strong internal culture and incorporating the market-based management philosophy is precisely to make the firm more responsive to the needs of customers and the innovations of competitors. With this in mind, Koch also remarked that "This kind of rapid response requires new ways of anticipating, discovering, and communicating customer desires to everyone in the organization from the sales force to the accounting staff."[12] The corporate culture that has evolved at Koch Industries as the result of the faithful and patient implementation of market-based management is a remarkable one indeed: Employee empowerment exists at every level in the firm, for Koch recognizes that every person in the organization plays an important role in the success of the business. Koch has very practical ways of driving fear out of the organization and enhancing creativity. For example, employees do not seek "promotions" and "raises" in the traditional sense, because they know that by using their abilities to the utmost, and through dedication and hard work that creates value for the firm, just rewards will follow. In general, the company has made a determined effort to get rid of red tape and bureaucratic barriers within the organization.

Koch Industries has developed a set of ten principles supporting the philosophy of market-based management that flows directly from the firm's mission statement and corporate philosophy. Koch's mission statement is a classic expression of the importance of creating value, as we use that expression in this book.

> MISSION: Maximize the present value of future profits to provide security and opportunity for stockholders and productive employees, which will also benefit our communities and society. Accomplish by building competitive advantages in better satisfying customer needs using less resources and by capturing profitable opportunities to satisfy customer needs and for investment. Create these advantages and opportunities through leadership in the development and practice of market-based management.[13]

Koch recognizes the value of profitability and the importance of stockholders as business realities, but its mission statement is truly multidimensional, and incorporates a stream of values.

The corporate philosophy that follows the mission statement begins with yet another expression of the paramount position that the creation of value has at Koch Industries (KII):

> PHILOSOPHY: Producing superior value for customers with less resources improves the viability of both KII and our customers, and the well-being in society. Only by striving to profit by this, the economic means, can we sustain our growth and continue to provide more and

better jobs. Our mission can best be accomplished when every employee contributes to these economic profits, which require a commitment to safe and environmentally sound practices. Thus, we strive to select, place, develop, reward, and provide security and opportunity for employees according to their contributions to the long-term profitability of KII.

Our success is determined primarily by how well we utilize our combined knowledge to anticipate and meet changing customer needs. Full use of this knowledge requires that we create a culture in which people are open and receptive, treat each other with care and respect, are provided the necessary education and information, and are given the opportunity to make meaningful contributions. We strive to transform our knowledge into profitable activity by improving decision-making processes, which includes clearly articulating individual responsibilities based on each person's comparative advantages, ensuring that everyone understands how his or her activities contribute to profits, and providing incentives for everyone to focus on advancing KII's mission.[14]

The ten principles follow logically from the company's mission statement and corporate philosophy, and each is in itself an important statement about creating value and the way Koch does business. The principles are: (1) conducting all business ethically and lawfully, (2) applying market-based management to improve profitability, (3) setting high expectations and developing critical-thinking skills and a risk-taking mentality, (4) developing better relationships with external and internal customers to anticipate and satisfy their needs, (5) developing and practicing humility and intellectual honesty, (6) treating others with dignity and respect to enable them to fully use their knowledge, (7) using and sharing the best knowledge in all decision making, (8) having the vision and openness to challenge the status quo, (9) engaging in continual learning and acceptance of change, and (10) having a ". . . compelling desire to create and produce such that work becomes a major focus of life."[15]

In the final section of this book we deal at length with how Value Driven Management can be implemented in an organization. Having a clear and multidimensional mission statement, an enlightened corporate philosophy, and a set of operating principles, based on the company mission and its philosophy, that all members of the organization led by the CEO believe, buy into, value, and practice (i.e., live), is a virtual precondition of implementation. At KII, the corporate culture is a powerful and positive force in creating value.

Unfortunately, it was the very lack of such values in the corporate culture of Texaco in 1994 that forced the company to later agree to pay $140 million to settle a racial discrimination case. At a meeting of senior executives during that year (which had been secretly taped), several company officers—including J. David Keough, the chief financial and administrative officer of a Bermuda subsidiary, and Peter Meade, an assistant general manager of Texaco's fuel and marine marketing unit—were heard using racial epithets to belittle African-American employees. When the tape was disclosed in 1996, major problems ensued, not surprisingly, because it was painfully obvious that such behavior was all too acceptable at high levels within Texaco.

African-American consumers angrily began boycotting Texaco gas stations throughout the United States. Saying that the company received bad publicity is understating the public reaction to the case. Even worse for Texaco, it was hit with a $520 million race-discrimination suit by six African-American plaintiffs, who alleged that the company systematically discriminated against minorities in hiring and promotion practices. After the disclosure of the tape, the company had little choice but to settle; especially when it suffered further embarrassment after the lawyers for the plaintiffs revealed that a survey carried out by Mobil Corporation showed that of all Texaco personnel earning $128,000 a year or more, only 0.4 percent were black, compared to 1.8 percent on average for other major American oil companies.[16]

Perhaps good sometimes does come out of bad, because in addition to paying the aforementioned $140 million to settle the case, Texaco agreed to purchase more services from minority-owned companies, established a five-year plan to significantly increase the presence of minorities at every level in the company, enrolled its 20,000 U.S. employees in diversity workshops, invested $420,000 to become the major sponsor of Universoul Big Top Circus—a black-owned circus—and increased its advertising in black-owned magazines.[17] The case is remarkable not only because of what it revealed about Texaco's internal culture, but because that culture's insensitivity to the external culture and to the firm's customers was so disastrous and immensely costly.

A positive example of internal culture is the one exemplified by flexibility and pride in productivity that has developed at the immensely successful low-fare airline company, Southwest Airlines, which is headed by one of America's most capable CEOs— the redoubtable Herb Kelleher. Southwest, and its dynamic internal culture, has been the subject of many analyses in management casebooks and textbooks. Authors Raymond Noe, John Hollenbeck, Barry Gerhart and Patrick Wright describe it this way:

> At Southwest, the organizational culture includes a high value on flexibility of the workforce. Employees take pride in their ability to get a plane ready to go in only 20 minutes, less than half the industry average. A cultural refrain is "Can't make money with the airplane sitting on the ground." Ramp agents unload baggage, clean the lavatories, carry out trash, and stock the plane with ice, drinks, and peanuts. Flight attendants prepare the cabin for the next flight, and pilots have been known to pitch in when they have time. Working hard is not just an obligation at Southwest; it is a source of pride. Ramp agent Mike Williams brags that in a conversation with an employee for another airline, the other man explained Southwest's fast turnaround by saying, in Williams' words, "The difference is that when one plane [the other company's] lands, they work it, and when one of our planes land, we *attack* it."[18]

While the productivity and work ethic in Southwest's culture is very well known, the sense of humor and hospitality that pervades the company—inspired by irrepressible CEO Kelleher—is

probably even more renowned. Kelleher is famous for the fact
that he values, and frequently uses, humorous jokes and anec-
dotes that would be an anathema to a more conventional executive. Stephanie Gruner comments in *Inc.* that:

> Few CEOs know how to whoop it up quite like Herb
> Kelleher. The irrepressible Kelleher, who in 1971 co-
> founded Southwest Airlines, has built a company in
> which impromptu celebrations are common. Sound
> frivolous? Quite the contrary, claims Kelleher. "What we
> do communicates itself to the outside world in better
> service and warmer hospitality," he says.[19]

So the humorous is also deadly serious, and has contributed to
the company's strong and continuous financial performance.
Newsweek's Daniel Pedersen notes that Southwest earned profits
of $433 million in 1998 from carrying 52.5 million passengers to
53 cities located primarily in the South and West.

> The average trip: 446 miles for $75. The so-called Wal-
> Mart of the Skies offers no assigned seats, no meals, no
> first class. Like its boss, it does have a bent sense of
> humor. Gate agents hold contests to see which traveler
> has the biggest hole in his sock. Kelleher has taped a
> rap number for new employees: "My name is Herb/Big
> Daddy-O/You should all know me/I run this show."[20]

Southwest's profitability and efficiency under Kelleher's leadership are no joke, however. The airline is arguably the best in its
industry, as judged by such indicators as on-time performance
and customer satisfaction with its service.

Kelleher's use of humor in the workplace is beguiling, but it
belies his outstanding ability to create value as Southwest's CEO.
In a *Harvard Business Review* article entitled "What Is Strategy?"
Michael Porter notes that the company has combined superb operational efficiency (it flies only Boeing 737 jets, for example, in
order to maximize safety and minimize costs) with a successful
long-term strategy of slow but steady growth on the short- to me-
dium-haul routes between the cities it serves.[21] Only recently has

it begun to compete with the so-called major carriers on longer routes in other regions of the country, and while its success in this venture is still uncertain as we write these words, the odds would seem to be in its favor. Its legendary culture of efficiency and good service should serve it as efficiently and well in its new markets as in its current ones.

Value Driver 3: Individual Employee Values

''When I was director of human resources at Koch Industries, we spent an incredible amount of time in employee selection on determining a prospective employee's personal values, since we wanted to know how well that person would fit into the company culture. I cannot think of a human resource strategy that created more value, or helped more in building our human assets.''—Randy A. Pohlman

Major corporations routinely spend millions and millions of dollars annually in the employee-selection process. Interviews are almost universally used, even though they typically have low reliability and poor validity. For example, women who are judged by male interviewers to be more, rather than less, attractive, are far more likely to receive a job offer, even when other factors are not equal. This so-called halo effect simply overwhelms other aspects of judgment. Reference and background checks are now quite routinely carried out to look for cases of resume falsification and cheating. Biographical information is almost always sought out on application forms, and can also be useful. Physical ability tests are used when a physical attribute such as strength or agility is a legitimate job qualification.

Cognitive ability tests let an organization know if a candidate is intellectually competent; personality inventories may screen out chronic problems that could be significant value destroyers on the job. Work sample tests effectively reveal whether or not that oh-so attractive candidate can actually carry out the job. Many companies now administer and have increasingly begun to use honesty tests. Organizations like Nordstrom, the upscale department store chain that we shall discuss again, are finding that the systematic use of such tests is useful in identifying employees who will stay with the organization.

> For example, Nordstrom's uses the Reid Survey to screen for violent tendencies, drug use, and dishonesty. Originally, the test was only one of many factors that went into the final hiring decision, so there were some people hired who were not recommended by the Reid test. Follow-up studies showed that the turnover rate for those recommended by the Reid test was only 22 percent, compared with 44 percent of those who did not pass the test but were hired anyway. Since the test cost only $5 to administer, this represents a major cost saving in the stores tested.[22]

In an industry where honesty and personal pleasantness are important qualities for success, Nordstrom's effective use of the Reid Survey is a good example of a proactive human-resource tactic that has helped the company match the values of those they are hiring against the values of the corporate culture.

Ability testing for job applicants now has a long history in human resource management, and it is obvious that such testing will continue to be a worthwhile and cost-effective practice in most industries. In the new millennium, however, it is a good bet that value testing and value congruency will become important themes in employee selection, organizational diagnosis, organizational productivity, and value creation. We have already briefly mentioned, that we feel value congruency will be recognized to be of critical importance by more and more organizations, and we also believe that it will be the subject of more and more research in the future. A growing body of research currently being conducted at Nova Southeastern University supports this view.

An early study by Robert Preziosi, professor of management in the Wayne Huizenga Graduate School of Business and Entrepreneurship, showed that there is a significant relationship between a set of high performance leadership values and organizational productivity.[23] The list of 20 high performance leadership values developed by Preziosi in previous work included such items as "build on success," "create newness," "measure everything," "embrace diversity," "offer learning resources," "provide equity in opportunity," "put others first," "use mental agility," "see the big picture," and "tap into teams." Each such value was clarified with a two- to three-sentence explanation of its meaning. His results were based on data supplied by 118 graduate students in management, chosen for ease of access from students who worked for numerous companies throughout Florida and the southeastern United States. Preziosi noted that while it is commonly accepted that one of a leader's top priorities is to set vision and values for their organization, his study is more tantalizing than conclusive since it did not attempt to determine the degree of congruency between the leader's and subordinate's values in the organizations in question.

In a follow-up study, Preziosi and his colleague, Pedro F. Pellet, associate professor of economics in the Huizenga School, began to address the issue of individual/organizational value consistency.[24] The subjects of the study (65 graduate students in management) were asked to complete the Value Analysis Worksheet and a Productivity Audit. The Value Analysis Worksheet is a Likert-type instrument that measures individual/organizational value consistency across 23 positive values such as loyalty, integrity, belief in high performance, and commitment to quality. The Productivity Audit is a 53-item measure that requires a "yes/no" response to a series of productivity leadership/management standards questions. Using a rank-order correlation procedure between the two sets of measures, Preziosi and Pellet discovered that they were strongly related, well beyond the .01 level of significance that is the commonly-accepted standard in scientific research (a less than one percent chance that the relationship is due to chance). In plain words, the less the value discrepancy between individuals and their organizations, the greater the productivity of the organization.

In a study designed to measure the impact of value congruence in a health care setting, Preziosi, Bill Harrington, professor of management in the Huizenga School, and doctoral student Jean Gordon studied the relationship between the critical-care nurses/hospital management values and perceived total quality management practices in a South Florida public hospital. Sixty-four critical-care nurses completed the Values Analysis Worksheet and a total quality management audit. Data analysis revealed a highly significant relationship between value consistency and the perception that total quality management was in place in the hospital: The closer the values of the nurses to the values of hospital administration, the stronger the perception that total quality management practices are used by the hospital.[25] In her dissertation research, Jean Gordon is investigating the hypothesis that there is a strong positive relationship between nurse/hospital value consistency, and the quality of health care in critical-care hospital settings. Her dissertation data strongly support this view.[26]

While a fairly substantial body of research indicates that value congruence is important to organizational success, the Nova Southeastern University research program is the first ongoing and large-scale investigation of the role of value congruence in different occupational settings. Not surprisingly, the values of key employees such as nurses and hospital administrators seem to matter. In the American retail industry, the experience of Seattle-based Nordstrom validates the importance of value congruence, as we shall see again in the detailed analysis that follows. Nordstrom has a 100-year history of empowering its sales associates, who are given virtually complete freedom to make the customer happy. This policy has become deeply imbedded in the company's culture—there is obviously a high degree of value congruence between the employees and management in this critical area—and the result has been the development of a truly phenomenal sales organization.

This value driver has major implications for both the organization and the individual. In making personnel selection decisions, the organization should strive to find those individuals whose values are congruent with those of the organization. This does not in any way mean that the principle of valuing diversity should be in any way short-changed, but what it does mean is that the individual being hired, and those already in the organization, will not be able to maximize value created for themselves and the organization if they do not fit the corporate culture.

Even though many managers and leaders are uncomfortable discussing the importance an individual has in the workplace, a growing body of research indicates that shared values in fact do create a framework within which employees make decisions and take action. This framework may have a very important impact on value creation for the organization. Randy Pohlman, who was head of human resources at Koch Industries (in a culture that valued and practiced employee empowerment), helped create a value-based prospective employee interview procedure to identify those persons whose personal values would enable them to fit into the company. This process was incredibly powerful in creating value in the development of Koch's human resource base. It sped up the assimilation of people into the company, and enhanced their ability to create value within a very short time-frame—to be extremely productive and motivated as a direct result of value congruence. It became clear during this process that not only did employees assimilate in the culture much more quickly, but that they were also much more highly motivated than employees in organizations that do not have a high degree of value congruence.

If an organization does not understand what its true value structure is, attempting to implement value congruence with its employees will be difficult at best. At Koch, most individuals who are hired are closely aligned with the company's philosophy, principles, and incentive structure, and they therefore tend to thrive in this type of environment.

In Pohlman's view, this value system has more to do with the success of Koch Industries than anyone outside of the company will ever realize. The firm's structure of strong ethical and moral values, functioning within the context of market-based management, has resulted in the phenomenal growth, profitability, and success of all of Koch's stakeholders—employees as well as owners.

Within the broader set of external cultural values and organizational cultural values, individuals have a complex spectrum of the things they value that affect the type of work they like to do, such as how they are supervised, how they are rewarded, and how they are motivated. We all have heard or have been heard saying, for example, that a particular individual has a very outgoing personality and likes to be "right out in front" and does excellent sales work. On the other hand, we sometimes refer to people as good "backroom" people. Such persons do not like to be in the limelight or interact frequently with other people, but prefer to be in the backroom doing technical work, sometimes working alone. Both types can create value in an appropriate organizational setting.

As research in the area of value congruence continues, it is likely that certain values and value-structures will become critical success factors (CSFs) in the employee selection process. One such set of values that was important at Koch was the assessment of a person's willingness to take responsibility for their own job satisfaction, to accept responsibility for becoming successful in the company, and in general, to avoid the "victim in life" syndrome that seems to afflict millions of American men and women. Clearly, willingness to accept responsibility was a CSF at Koch, just as it obviously is at Nordstrom, and was at Johnson & Johnson during the Tylenol-poisoning crisis. Willingness to accept responsibility is so important in organizational life, and to the maximization of value over time, that it may become *the* defining variable in the proactive, strategic and successful organizations of the future.

Los Angeles-based psychologist and consultant Nathaniel Branden, in his book *Taking Responsibility*, spoke about responsibility this way:

> Too often the idea of self-responsibility is interpreted to mean the taking on of new weights and obligations. It is equated with drudgery. Yet operating self-responsibly may entail saying no to burdens one never should have accepted in the first place. Many people find it easier to say yes to unreasonable requests than to stand up for their own interests. Taking on responsibilities that properly belong to someone else means behaving irresponsibly toward oneself. All of us need to know where we end and someone else begins; we need to understand boundaries. We need to know what is and is not up to us, what is and is not within our control, and what is and is not our responsibility. In coming to understand what self-responsibility and independence mean and do not mean, we see that they are essential to personal fulfillment, basic to a moral life, and the foundation of so-

cial cooperation. We see that the conventional tendency to cast individualism as the enemy of community and culture rests on a profound misunderstanding.[27]

Responsible people work in, and help build, responsible and prosperous organizations because their willingness to accept responsibility—and their unwillingness to blame others when things go wrong—is a powerful and constructive message to every employee in every organization. O. C. Ferrell and Gary Gardiner commented on this fact in a business ethics book, *In Pursuit of Ethics*:

> Taking responsibility is a powerful act, psychologically and emotionally. It communicates all sorts of good and helpful things to those around you. It lets people know that you are human, ethical, and honest, and that you want to get the problem solved. Taking responsibility does two additional things: It improves relationships among people who must work together to solve the problem, and it reduces anxiety in the entire organization. It helps create an environment where people can begin to give up defensive behaviors and begin to deal with problems in a more open and honest way.[28]

When employees at every level in the organization behave in this way, the outcome is increased trust throughout the firm, and trust is the glue that holds healthy and value-creating organizations together. Writing in *Organizational Dynamics*, professor and management consultant W. Alan Randolph remarks matter of factly that "Bureaucratic organizations are typically close to bankruptcy in terms of trust. As a result, people exert enormous energy in trying to protect themselves."[29] In bureaucratic and reactive organizations, decisions are often made in secrecy by the people at the top, the books are closed to the average employee, and people and their competencies are devalued as they wallow in an atmosphere of fear. Such organizations are not only typically close to bankruptcy in trust, they are often also close to just plain old bankruptcy.

Value Driver 4: Customer Values

''Value reigns supreme in today's marketplace where customers will no longer pay more than a good or service is worth. Consider the remarkable success of service organizations such as Amazon.com, Dell Computer, General Electric, Hewlett-Packard, Lexus, Motorola, Nordstrom, Inc., Rubbermaid, Southwest Airlines, and Wal-Mart—these companies truly know to maximize value for their customers.''—Art Weinstein and Bill Johnson, professors of marketing, Wayne Huizenga Graduate School of Business and Entrepreneurship, Nova Southeastern University, writing in their new book, *Designing and Delivering Superior Customer Value: Concepts, Cases, and Applications.*

Many readers may agree that mantras have their uses in understanding management and the process of creating value, and the mantra that it has become a customer-driven world, or globe, is just such a truism. No successful organization or firm in this globalized world can lose sight of what its customers want and remain a successful organization or, for that matter, stay in business over the long haul.

Management guru Tom Peters and his coauthor Robert Waterman brought this fact into focus in the early 1980s with the publication of a work that has gone on to become a true business classic, if not a mantra, in the years since its appearance: *In Search of Excellence.*[30] The book identified some of America's best companies—Merck, Rubbermaid, Dow Jones, Procter & Gamble, Liz Claiborne, 3M, Phillip Morris, RJR Nabisco, Wal-Mart, IBM (now rejuvenated and resourceful), L. L. Bean, American Express, McDonald's, Johnson & Johnson, and Hewlett-Packard, to name several—and asked the questions, "What makes them excellent? What things do they do that set them apart from run-of-the-mill or unsuccessful firms?" Now, we must confess that the book did not *literally* ask these questions, but it is fair to say that this is what *In Search of Excellence* is all about—the criteria that distinguish the best from the rest.

Early on, Peters and Waterman note that the best companies make a great effort to select and hire the right people, to expend resources on training them not only adequately but to expand their skills across narrow job boundaries, to find creative ways to motivate and keep them on board, to give them adequate authority to both do their jobs and do their jobs well. The importance of human assets and the empowerment of those assets is truly a given for excellent organizations. These firms also value their relationships with their customers highly, and often find creative ways to stay in touch with customers, such as soliciting regular and continuing feedback from customers. According to O. C. Ferrell and Geoffrey Hirt, "They invest in technology to support customer service and they keep enough supplies on hand to meet customer and employee needs. Many involve customers in the product development process to ensure that products do what customers need them to do."[31]

Like other great books in every field of human endeavor, *In Search of Excellence* has truly been a prescient volume: Peters and Waterman anticipated the rising power of customer values and customer service. Art Weinstein, professor of marketing at Nova Southeastern University, and Randy Pohlman note that creating and enhancing customer value has emerged as a dominant theme for business success in the 1990s.

> Value may be an "old" concept, but it is a new imperative in business. Value is the strategic driver that multinational planners utilize (sic) as well as innovative entrepreneurs to differentiate themselves from the pack in the mind of the customer. Value means many things to many people. How is it that Lexus can sell automobiles for $50,000 and Taco Bell can offer meal combos for less than $3 and both are good values? Value is defined by the customer! Naumann explains that the customer value triad consists of three key ingredients: value-based prices, product quality, and service quality. Varying emphases on these elements explicates a company's value proposition. As an example, Wal-Mart stresses low price, Hewlett-Packard is obsessed with new product development and the quality of its products, and Nordstrom is renowned for superior customer service.[32]

Delivering superior customer value can also give a firm a long run and a sustainable competitive advantage. Obtaining and maintaining such an advantage, not surprisingly, requires an integrated and multidimensional management approach.

In the long run, a sustainable competitive advantage (SCA) requires the integration of the voices of the customer, the competition, and the firm. Outstanding business performance is dependent on the ability of a market-oriented firm to provide the maximum value to the customer. This can be accomplished via a business culture that stresses world-class service, quality improvement, and new product innovation.[33]

The concept of the *value funnel* (see Figure 5-1) captures and summarizes the dual foundation of business performance: (1) anticipating and responding to the *relevant values* of all eight of the constituencies of the organization—this is a reference, of course, to the eight value drivers we have been discussing, and (2) "value maximisation (sic)—how economic value and knowledge is created throughout an organisation (sic) to best serve its target customers."[34] The four levels of the funnel—which are interdependent, and viewed from a broad to narrow lens—illustrate a downward flow of decisional processes, but the feedback loops in levels I, II, and III ". . . demonstrate that market intelligence is an ongoing, iterative, interactive, and integrated process. If business performance does not meet corporate objectives, strategic or tactical changes are mandated."[35] In short, the firm that seeks to create customer value must be value driven, strategic, and proactive; terms that our readers are by now familiar with.

In their new book, *Designing and Delivering Superior Customer Value: Concepts, Cases, and Applications,*[36] Art Weinstein and Bill Johnson elaborate upon these ideas. They focus on the importance of retaining customers through the use of relationship marketing and designing a comprehensive customer-retention program; identifying service quality and finding ways to improve quality; developing a customer-oriented organizational culture; and using strategic marketing management to create product/service value.

Figure 5-1 The value funnel.

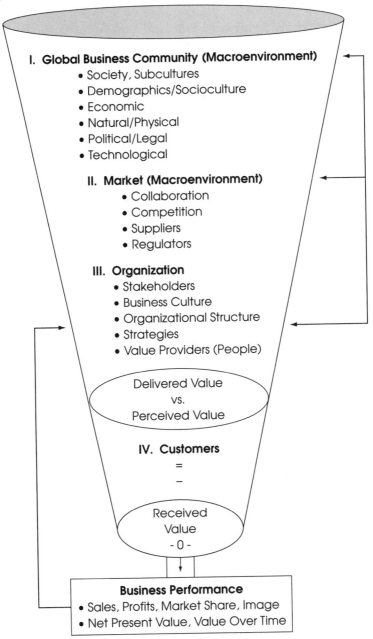

A company that has become legendary for its service quality and its loving attention to the needs of customers, is Nordstrom which is currently headed by Pete and Dan Nordstrom—fourth-generation family members who took command in 1995 and serve as copresidents of the operation (along with three other family members). According to Seattle writers Robert Spector and Patrick D. McCarthy, authors of a 1996 book entitled *The Nordstrom Way*, the company has such a legendary reputation for service and sales that other retailers virtually panic when the word spreads that Nordstrom is planning to build a new outlet in their area.

> Employees are rounded up and told they will have to start giving "Nordstrom-style" service: salespeople are ordered to smile, to be nice to the customers, and to scribble "thank you" on the sales receipt, because, "That's the way the Nordstrom sales people act." These retailers have little hope of ever approaching Nordstrom's legendary service and sales, because Nordstrom's way of treating customers is not an "act" that salespeople turn on and off. It's part of a deeply imbedded culture that has taken the Nordstrom family nearly 100 years and four generations to perfect.[37]

Spector and McCarthy note that Nordstrom has a long history of profitability, and that its annual sales per square foot of floor space are about $400, nearly twice the industry average.

These authors argue throughout *The Nordstrom Way* that the company's success is the direct result of management's strong support of a focus on building a long-term relationship with the customer, which is also one of the central arguments in Weinstein's and Johnson's book on creating customer value. Nordstrom's customer orientation has become an integral part of its corporate culture say Spector and McCarthy, and they identify some of the key concepts of that culture:

- Salespeople are truly empowered to make decisions to serve the customer in any way they believe will make her happy.
- Sales associates are encouraged to build their own busi-

nesses within the company—and generous commissions reward them for what they add to the bottom line.

- Nordstrom's wide variety makes sure the salesperson never has to turn away a customer because a style or size isn't available.
- The store's unconditional return policy helps associates to sell merchandise, because every purchase is risk-free.
- The company's store design is carefully planned to make the shopping experience enjoyable and comfortable, so shoppers are in no hurry to leave.
- Employees and managers are under strict orders from top management to think of the customer's desires first, and the company's costs second.
- All store managers, department managers, and buyers are promoted from within—and all start in the stock room or on the sales floor.
- Profit-sharing plans give employees an incentive to prevent shrinkage.[38]

Nordstrom's century-long emphasis on customer satisfaction and values has led to the development of a powerful mystique, and to the rise of company legends—true stories of incredible examples of customer service. At least two of these stories, as recounted by Spector and McCarthy, are well worth repeating here.

- A customer asked a sales associate for a pair of slacks that were on sale, but the associate discovered that the store had run out of her size. After calling other Nordstrom stores in the area, she still couldn't deliver what the customer wanted. So the associate bought the slacks from a competing department store across the street. Though she had to pay the other store's full price, the associate charged the customer the sale price.
- A customer wrote to a sales associate to say that the $2,000 in shirts he had purchased had shrunk when they were mistakenly washed in hot water. The customer admitted the error was his own, and asked for advice. The associate called the customer and told him he was replacing the shirts at no charge.[39]

The authors note that in all of the "heroic" sales acts that they document in their book, not one of the salespersons involved ever had to ask a manager for permission to do what they had. Nordstrom not only preaches empowerment, it practices it. In fact, the company's employee "handbook" comfortably fits a five-by-eight inch card, since it consists of two short statements: "Rule #1: Use your good judgment in all situations. There will be no additional rules."

The Nordstrom legend is not only supported by internal stories of extraordinary service such as the ones we have recounted here, it is also validated by the experiences of hundreds of thousands of Americans who have enjoyed service far and beyond the call of duty as Nordstrom customers. When Randy Polhman was on a business trip to San Francisco, he found himself in a Nordstrom store, looking at a pair of shoes that the store did not have in his size. After telling the sales associate of his wish to buy a pair of shoes in that style, but that would fit, she immediately began calling other stores to see if a properly-sized pair was available. Within two hours, the associate left a voice-mail message at his hotel—as promised—that the shoes were available at the store for pick up.

When he returned to pick up his shoes, he happened to mention that he had purchased another pair of shoes from Nordstrom about a year earlier and that a problem had developed with the soles. The associate immediately asked him to leave the shoes with her, saying she would take care of the problem. She said the same thing she had earlier: she would leave a voice-mail message at his hotel. Within hours, the message was left; and the beautifully-repaired shoes were available at the store for pick up.

But the story does not end at this point. When he returned to the store to pick up the shoes, the associate inquired whether or not he would be interested in picking up a pair of shoe trees that were priced at about $20. After being told, politely, that he was not interested in a pair of shoetrees at just this moment, she thoughtfully mentioned that the shoe trees would be going on sale a few months later—in June—and that she would be willing to contact him in Wichita, Kansas, if he would like to take advantage of the sale. Not really believing that anyone would go out of the way to let a customer know about a shoetree sale, he expressed this thought verbally. "I really don't expect you to go out of the way like that." "Oh, I will, sir," she replied.

Amazingly, or perhaps normally at Nordstrom, Pohlman was sitting at his desk in Wichita several months later and the phone rang. It was the Nordstrom sales associate in San Francisco, calling to advise him that the shoetrees were on sale, and asking if he would like to buy a pair. Despite his consternation at the fact the associate had actually kept her promise and remembered to call him, he bought not one, but *two* pairs of the shoetrees at the bargain price.

Such stories are the stuff of legend, as we have already noted, but Nordstrom's almost obsessive focus on creating customer value—as expressed in every aspect of the firm's culture—has created tremendous value for Nordstrom. The company has now expanded out of its traditional Pacific Northwest base, and has more than 75 stores located in just about every major metropolitan area in the nation. Nordstrom is truly one of America's excellent companies.

Value Driver 5: Supplier Values

"To build more flexible and efficient supply chains, manufacturers need to forge close, long-term ties with suppliers. They need to work hand in hand to refine products and components, respond to shifts in demand, and unclog bottlenecks, all the time sharing sensitive information."—John T. Landry, writing in *Harvard Business Review*.

The traditional mindset about suppliers, as we have already noted, tends to be that they bring up the rear in the value creation chain, as well as bringing up the rear in the production and manufacturing chain. Traditionally, the eager and humble supplier was at the beck and call of the imperious and sometimes arrogant manufacturer: suppliers lined up, hat in hand, to accept whatever contract the producer might choose to offer on a given day. It was a one-way street. Naturally, this stereotype of supplier/producer relationships has always been far too simplistic, although it undoubtedly had a grain of truth in it. The rise of the global economy has completely shattered another old file folder, of course, and the emergence of new and dynamic relationships between suppliers and manufacturers has been one of the most surprising developments of the new multidimensional world of business. Supplier relationships and values have never been more important in the business-production chain and to the process of creating value over time, as a recent editorial briefing in *Harvard Business Review* makes clear.

In a piece entitled "Supply Chain Management: The Case for Alliances," John Landry summarizes important research by Paul Lawrence of the Harvard Business School and Ranjay Gulati of the J. L. Kellogg Graduate School of Management, Northwestern University, who studied supply relationships at Chrysler (now DaimlerChrysler) and Ford.[40] The findings of these two researchers suggest that *trust* is a critical criterion of relationships between suppliers and manufacturers, and that high-trust relationships can be achieved through alliances with outside suppliers if both parties work hard to develop a collaborative relationship. These authors note that it has always been assumed that high levels of trust could only be developed with internal suppliers, but it is now clear that alliances with external partners can be just as trusting as—and even more efficient and productive than—when a company relies exclusively on internal units.

Four conditions seem to be important in building win-win relationships with external suppliers:

1. *Power balancing.* The traditional notion of a powerful buyer, like Wal-Mart, using its leverage to extract concessions from a supplier is giving way to a more balanced relationship in which neither party is highly dependent on the other. "Such power balancing does more than make suppliers feel less vulnerable—it also helps the manufacturer. Suppliers become more innovative as they work with and learn from other customers, and the manufacturer reaps the benefits of the suppliers' greater creativity."[41] Landry also notes that breaking away from the traditional power and dominance mindset is vital to the development of a trusting and consultative relationship.

2. *Cospecialization.* By nominating "preferred suppliers" for certain components, manufacturers encourage suppliers to

make contributions to the design and engineering of these components. This process of cospecialization reaches a zenith in so called modular plants, which are now being pioneered in the auto industry by DaimlerChrysler, Volkswagen, Ford, and General Motors, and which we shall discuss further.

3. *Target costing.* Target costing is also a cooperative system where the purchasing manager sets a target price for a component, and encourages the supplier to engage in a joint problem-solving process in increased design and production efficiency.

4. *Personalities.* Professors Lawrence and Gulati found that people make all the difference in managing supply chains.

Relationships among managers are often what keep alliances productive; for example, the establishment of joint teams to solve problems not only improves the flow of information, but also encourages each side to feel comfortable with the other. The trust resulting from such interpersonal bonding significantly reduces the need for "cumbersome" legal contracts as the partners become more comfortable in doing business with each other.

Ranjay Gulati sums it up nicely in Landry's *Harvard Business Review* editorial briefing:

> Manufacturers often get the better of two worlds when they form strong supplier alliances. They get to work with independent, flexible companies able to specialize in a given component, and they also achieve the close integration thought to be possible only with in-house divisions.

"Indeed," Gulati adds, "manufacturers that spun off supply units were pleasantly surprised to find that these suppliers greatly improved their business practices."[42]

The emergence of strong manufacturer/supplier alliances is the logical culmination of a trend that has emerged not only in the auto industry, but in other industries as well, and that trend is *outsourcing.* Outsourcing, the procurement of supplies and components from independent outside contractors and companies, rather than from in-house divisions or units, is a development that has been driven by two imperatives emerging from the rise of the global economy: the need for timely delivery of high-quality components and parts, and the need to reduce costs in the face of intense competitive pressures. The advocates of outsourcing argue that it has simply become a necessity in an era of complex and specialized production processes, where meeting rigorous quality standards and criteria is a condition of staying in business. Its critics complain that it is just another attempt on the part of manufacturers to get rid of high-cost, unionized labor, and to replace that labor with low-cost, nonunion labor. The development of so-called modular plants in the auto industry may prove to be a definitive test case.

Writing in *Business Week*, Kathleen Kerwin notes that modular plants in the auto industry have appeared mainly in emerging markets like Brazil, where several major manufacturers—including Volkswagen, Chrysler, and Ford—already have such plants. According to Kerwin, "Modular assembly is, at heart, an extension of outsourcing, the common practice of buying parts from outside suppliers. For years, auto makers have been shifting away from producing most of a car's 5,000 components by contracting parts, or even groups of them, to suppliers."[43] In modular plants, outsourcing has been developed to a new extreme: Suppliers design and develop an entire chunk of the car—the chunk is called a module—and then provide the completed module to the manufacturer. The suppliers set up their plants next to the manufacturer's plant or, as is the case with Volkswagen's new plant in Brazil, right inside the automaker's plant.

Understandably, auto industry executives are strong advocates of the concept. Former Chrysler Chairman Robert Eaton argues that it is impossible for any auto company to carry out, in-house, all of the R & D and other development needed to manufacture today's complex vehicles, while former Daimler Benz marketing director Dieter Zetsche adds, "That modular assembly leads to more efficient designs with fewer parts." Mike Laisure of Dana Corporation (an auto parts maker) believes that outsourcing companies can get the job done more quickly.[44] Of the major auto manufacturers, General Motors has the strongest incentive to implement modular assembly, since it has by far the highest production costs of any member of this group, particularly on its money-losing small car lines.

In a classic clash of values, GM is anticipating strong opposition from a third party—the United Auto Workers—in developing its first modular plants in this country. One of the attractions for automakers in countries like Brazil has been the lack of union opposition to the development of innovative modular technology. In the United States, the UAW has generally been bitterly opposed to outsourcing, and is likely to rise in wrath against the development of American modular plants, fearing a wholesale loss of union jobs. GM claims that it will largely handle job shrinkage through attrition, but it has already endured costly strikes over just this issue.[45]

The creation and maintenance of good supplier relationships is crucial to the success of many organizations. Decisions made or actions taken must be carefully considered when suppliers may be affected. Issues affecting suppliers could range from decisions or actions affecting the people who work with them, to the procedures or systems they work with. Suppliers' reactions must be carefully analyzed, and the anticipated impact on VOT must be calculated prior to any action being taken or decision made.

It is perhaps inevitable that these new and creative forms of supply-chain management will also create new forms of stress and conflict, but it is also inevitable that creative and value-driven organizations will continue to develop such initiatives, given the continuing global imperative for more efficient and cost-effective production. Watch for even more change in this area, not less.

Value Driver 6: Third-Party Values

``To be sure, no corporation can sustain itself without appropriate attention to all those who hold a stake in its performance: customers certainly, but also suppliers, creditors, neighbors, society in general and, of course, those most directly affected—employees. Companies are infinitely better equipped to respond sensibly to today's pressures on behalf of all the stakeholders—before the `one-size-fits-all' feds do it for them. . . . And in the end, embracing voluntary changes in

> corporate governance is nothing more than enlightened self-interest. Taking action now can pay off for the shareowners and *all* the stakeholders.''—Richard J. Mahoney, former CEO, Monsanto Company, writing in *The CEO Series*.

One of the enduring and endearing images in Ken Burns' PBS series on the American Civil War is a picture of a group of Union soldiers playing baseball while idle between battles. Baseball has long been referred to as the nation's pastime, and during the first two-thirds of the twentieth century it held a virtually unchallenged position as the country's most popular sport, even after the rise of football and basketball as rivals. Despite the huge popularity of stars like Babe Ruth, Dizzy Dean, Lou Gehrig, and Joe DiMaggio in the early and middle years of the century, and the breaking of the so-called color line in 1947 when the multitalented Jackie Robinson joined the Brooklyn Dodgers, there was no question who dominated the sport—the owners did. A number of attempts at player unionization eventually led to the rise of the Major League Players' Association, and to a change in the balance of power in the game.

The players' association, or union, soon negotiated better working conditions for the players, such as better scheduling and more generous meal allowances, but its major impact was on salaries, including the development of free agency in 1977, which did away with a system that had bound players to their teams unless they were traded or waived by the team to which they were under contract. The rise in the minimum annual salary of major-league players was dramatic: it went from $6,000 in 1967, to $200,000 in 1999. Free-agent salaries escalated rapidly, and by the 1990s newly signed free agents were routinely earning multi-million-dollar salaries.

Despite a players' strike in 1972, which delayed the start of the season, and another in 1981, which resulted in a split season (neither of which caused the cancellation of the World Series), the popularity of the game continued at a very high level. During the 1994 season, attendance per major-league game reached an all-time high, until disaster struck—along with the players. A long-simmering labor dispute, largely over economic considerations, led to a player walkout in August, the cancellation of the rest of the season, and—worst—the cancellation of the 1994 World Series. The result of this classic clash of value drivers—a third party in the form of the militant players' union, the owners eager to win and unwilling to significantly share revenues, and loyal fans who now had many other choices of sports to watch—resulted in destruction of value for the entire industry for years to come.

Attendance plummeted in 1995. Per game attendance dropped about 25 percent compared to the 1994 season, and ratings for televised games were also down significantly. Fans were perhaps most disgusted with the players, whom many regarded as spoiled and overpaid, but the owners shared almost equally in earning their displeasure.

Fans suspected, rightly, that their long-time loyalty to the game had come to be taken for granted. The sport recovered somewhat in the seasons that followed, but as late as 1998, attendance per game had still not reached pre-strike levels, and the television ratings for the 1998 World Series, in which the New York Yankees defeated the San Diego Padres four games to none, were dismally low. The most exciting home run race in the history of the game, in which the St. Louis Cardinals' Mark McGwire outdueled the Chicago Cubs' Sammy Sosa 70 home runs to 66, disguised the fact that attendance was down for about half the teams. According to syndicated columnist George Will, one of the country's most ardent admirers of the game of baseball but a severe critic of the industry, fans had caught on to the fact that economic disparities in the game had finally made it virtually impossible for teams in small markets like Pittsburgh, Minnesota, and Montreal to have any chance of winning.

In a column written prior to the start of the 1999 season, entitled "The Trouble With Modern-Day Baseball," Will took note of the competitive imbalance in major league baseball, which he attributes in large part to the unwillingness of owners in large markets (including George Steinbrenner of the Yankees) to engage in significant sharing of revenues with small-market teams. Said Will:

> Sports leagues have rules to contrive competitive balance. The aim is not to guarantee equal revenues, but

revenues sufficient to give each team periodic chances
of winning if each uses its revenues intelligently. Baseball's rules no longer suffice. . . . Under free agency,
1978-87 was the first 10-year span in which 10 different
teams won the World Series. Attendance, broadcast revenues and new ballpark construction had boomed. But
now revenue disparities have widened to the point that
about 20 of the 30 teams were virtually excluded from
this winter's market for premier free agents. What has
changed? Local broadcast revenues have become more
important and more unequal. (The Yankees get $55 mil-
lion, the Royals $5 million.)[46]

Clearly both the owners and the players must share the blame
for baseball's problems, but the plight of the industry is the result
of critically-important value drivers that were not weighed heavily
enough in the resolution of disputes, most significantly the values
of its customers—the baseball fans of America.

Most other sports, including basketball and football, have
worked out revenue-sharing formulas that promote more competitive equality than does baseball, even though other sports
have also endured their own player strikes or lockouts. Their
stakeholders and decision makers have recognized that value
creation is heavily dependent on ensuring that a majority of the
teams have at least some chance of winning if the fans are to keep
coming—a field of dreams is a vital ingredient, it seems, in the
psychology of nearly every sports fan.

Alas, the baseball industry, including the owners and the
players, is not yet this enlightened, and so the prognosis for the
future of baseball is still clouded. Third-party values, such as
those of governments, labor unions, and regulators often create
great conflict in business decision making because they so often
clash with the economic and other interests of owners and other
constituents of the business. Often it seems that an organizational
decision maker must have the wisdom of King Solomon in order
to make the right choices in situations like the baseball players'
strike of 1994, the 1998 lockout of the National Basketball Association players by the owners, or the "sick-out" by American Airlines' pilots early in 1999 that angered hundreds of thousands of

American's customers left stranded at airports. The pilots were concerned about the fact that American's buyout of discount carrier Reno Air—which was nonunionized, and whose pilots made significantly less than at American—would lead to lower wages for them, even though contract negotiations were some time away. The question that was largely begged during the extensive media coverage of the sick-out was what the company could have done to prevent the pilots from staging their illegal walkout. Knowing that the union pilots might be anxious about their economic future, could management have taken action to prevent the walkout?

Such proactive and preventive action should not require the wisdom of a King Solomon, but from the point of view of Value Driven Management it *does* require that a well-run business consider the potential destructiveness of what third parties value in its decision-making processes. Richard J. Mahoney, whom we quoted at length to introduce this section, has addressed this very issue in a *CEO Series* essay entitled "Business Should Act for All Its Stakeholders—Before 'The Feds' Do."[47] The title is a dead giveaway. Mahoney argues that enlightened businesses will take voluntary action when government regulation of industry may be pending, rather than after the fact. He notes that between 1970 and 1996, federal regulatory agencies' budgets more than *tripled*—from $5.2 billion to $16 billion—as measured in constant 1995 dollars. This greatly increased level of funding was also accompanied by a host of new federal regulatory programs.

> These programs ranged from hiring and promotion practices, directed benefits and worker safety rules, to minority purchasing standards, and a host of others. The results were felt by industry and the public—for example, effectively even dictating the size of automobiles based on fuel economy standards. A degree of this regulatory outburst may well have represented an appropriate response to the wishes of the public. But much was wasteful and counterproductive. Of course, it was ultimately paid for by the people themselves, in higher prices—presumably more palatable than higher taxes.[48]

He argues that business should not simply acquiesce to pending legislation and get ready, but instead—in the words of all-time goal scoring hockey great Wayne Gretzky, giving advice on how to score goals—business should "skate to where the puck *will be*, not where it is now."[49]

Value Driver 7: Owner Values

> "Similarly, I believe it would be wrong, perhaps even arrogant, for a business to think it can be all things to all people. We have one job: to generate a fair return for our owners, who have entrusted their assets to us. Without focusing on that job, we fail. And an unfocused, unsuccessful company not only fails to deliver value to its owners, it is a drag on the rest of society. Healthy companies, by contrast, can contribute to society in a wide variety of ways."— the late Roberto C. Goizueta, former Chairman and CEO of the Coca-Cola Company, writing in *The CEO Series*.

As a former professor of finance, Randy Pohlman vividly recalls that for years business school courses in finance were taught with an almost exclusive emphasis on "the maximization of shareholders' wealth." This approach to the subject was based on all-too-typical unidimensional thinking, in this case an erroneous assumption that the shareholders of a company are the only important constituents it has. Since the shareholders, or owners, have put up their money (invested in the company) they are, therefore, entitled to everything they can get. This theory is based on the notion that the shareholders are so-called residual owners, who get what is left over after all the other constituents of the organization are satisfied or "squared with."

After suppliers are paid, customers served, regulators satisfied, employees and other providers of capital paid, and cultural norms adhered to, the owners finally get what is left over, if anything, as a reward for their investment. They are deserving of this just reward, the theory holds, since they risked their hard-earned funds by investing in the company. Further, if they fail to receive a return on their investment that is commensurate with the risk they have taken, they will no longer invest in the firm or liquidate their existing holdings and move on. They are investing in the company on a short-term basis, and have no other interest in the firm except the money they have at stake.

Is this view fundamentally correct? The answer is a bold and unequivocal "yes" and "no." Many investors in a firm, including institutional investors like pension-fund managers, do indeed have a short-term stake in the organization because they must answer to the funds they are managing money for. When institutional investors own a significant share of a publicly traded company's stock, there will often be heavy pressure on the firm's CEO and its executive team to maximize short-term returns.

But, is the almost-addictive devotion to short-term profitability a sensible and wise way to manage a corporation in the long run? The late Roberto Goizueta of Coca-Cola spoke to this point, and eloquently, during his lifetime.

> Think about it. If a company wanted merely to create shareowner value *right now*, its leaders could suddenly make hundreds of decisions that would deliver a staggering short-term windfall. They could gouge their customers and suppliers. They could stop investing in their brands or stop behaving like good corporate citizens. They could slash salaries and benefits. They could put their business up for auction to the highest bidder. But that type of behavior has nothing to do with sustaining value creation over time.[50]

Goizueta points out in the same piece that creating value over the long haul means making yourself of unique value to your consumers, customers, partners, and fellow employees. Before his death from lung cancer on October 18, 1997, at the age of 65, Goizueta engineered an unprecedented 16-year period of profitability and productivity at Coca-Cola, which resulted in a nearly fortyfold increase in the company's value during his long and successful tenure as its CEO.

The *Corporate Observer*, published by the Hispanic Association on Corporate Responsibility, eulogized him this way:

> Goizueta's leadership helped the company expand its market value from $4 billion in 1981 to nearly $150 bil-

lion today. His tenure was marked by a host of bold, often stunning moves. During his 16 years at the helm, the company introduced Diet Coke and "new" Coke, and created significant, successful businesses in the previously untapped regions of China, Russia, and India. The company also contributed nearly $100 million to educational initiatives around the world.[51]

He not only understood the power of Value Driven Management, he practiced it faithfully over the long haul. It is clear that history will judge him kindly, as one of the most enlightened CEOs ever to head a major American company.

Richard J. Mahoney, former Chairman and CEO of Monsanto Company, has also addressed this issue, like Goizueta, writing in *The CEO Series* in a piece provocatively titled, "The Shareowner's Voice: Are We 'Listening to Prozac'?" When he assumed the leadership of Monsanto he was faced with a dilemma.

Like many newly minted CEOs, I asked the eternal question: "Who is it I represent? Employees? Customers? Neighbors? Society in general?" A voice sounding suspiciously like economic guru Milton Friedman thundered back in reply: "All of them and some more—but don't ever, *ever* forget the shareowners or *you'll* be forgotten. Listen to the shareowners—they own the company."[52]

Mahoney had done his homework when he became Monsanto's CEO in 1983. He knew that the dozen or so Wall Street analysts who would "opine" on whether or not he was delivering value to the firm's stockholders would define his success in terms of "no earnings surprises" and "the future is *now*."

In his 12 years as the company's CEO, however, he learned that he had to listen to the voices of *all* of Monsanto's constituents: ". . . employees, suppliers, neighbors, indeed, society in general—all of whom provide the "license to operate."[53] Nonetheless, in a company two-thirds owned by institutional investors, he felt terrible pressure to perform for the managers of these funds, since "these money managers have enormous pressures put on *them* to perform for the *real* owners—pensioners, 401K employee investors, and others."[54] He notes that missing an analyst's quarterly or yearly earnings forecast will get you plenty of bad ink, but he wryly remarks that if these voices are the only ones the CEO listens to, and if he slavishly follows their advice, it is like "listening to Prozac"—it feels good until the effect wears off.

Fortunately for them, the CEOs of privately-held companies are not subject to the same ferocious short-term financial pressures that the CEOs of public firms must endure, particularly when they and their families are major stockholders. Charles Koch of Koch Industries and his brother David own almost all of the company's stock, as do Bob Haas and his family of Levi Strauss & Company. Although it may be easier for such leaders to adopt and maintain a strategic and visionary leadership style, the fact that they are insulated to some extent from the expectations that public CEOs face, in no way protects them from the necessity to run their businesses intelligently and soundly. As we have already noted, Levi Strauss discovered this fact, and painfully, in the late 1990s as it lost market share to other apparel manufacturers who seemed more in touch with the sometimes fickle market for blue jeans and other lines of casual clothing, it was forced to close plants and lay off thousands of loyal and long-time employees and virtually cease production of garments in this country.

While institutional investors own huge chunks of some of our largest publicly held corporations, and are often criticized for having a very short-term perspective on the creation of value, some of the nation's many successful firms—like Coca-Cola—have a fairly broad ownership base; there is no question that this is a contributing factor to their ability to maintain a more strategic, long-term, and proactive orientation. In his 1997 *CEO Series* article entitled "Why Shareowner Value?" Coca-Cola's Goizueta notes that nearly 18 percent of the company is owned by employees, 38 percent by institutional investors, 36 percent by individuals (many of whom have held their stock for decades), and 8 percent by charities, endowments, and foundations.[55] This ownership structure is significantly more diverse and broad-based than that of many other large companies, which are often 80 to 90 percent owned by institutions.

This thought returns us to a 1998 book that we have mentioned earlier, *The Ownership Solution*, written by lawyer, investment banker, political advisor, and management consultant Jeff
Gates. The book's major premise is that extensive institutional
ownership of major companies is turning them into financial vehicles for passive investors; this phenomenon is leading to a serious decline in corporate stewardship and social responsibility,
as well as creating dramatic inequalities of wealth and power in
nations all over the globe. The rise of capitalistic democracies
throughout the world has been accompanied, and stimulated, by
the emergence of a strong middle class in every such nation—a
middle class that actively consumes goods and services, that is
active in the nation's political process, and that invests in the
companies that it works for. If Gates is correct and the world is
becoming a two-class society, consisting of the haves and have-
nots, there are ominous implications for the future of democratic
capitalism.

The Ownership Solution outlines a series of steps for broadening ownership, and one of Gates' principal recommendations
is expanding the reach of employee ownership through ESOPs,
or employee stock ownership plans. ESOPs have grown steadily
in popularity throughout the 1990s, and by the end of 1998, according to the ESOP Association headquartered in Washington,
D.C., there were approximately 10,000 companies in the United
States with ESOPs, covering about ten million employees, or 10
percent of the workforce.[56] In 1974, there were only 250 ESOPs in
this country, and the percentage of corporate equity owned by
employees at that time was insignificant. By 1997, however, the
National Center for Employee Ownership reported that approximately 9 percent of all corporate equity in the United States
(about $8 trillion in that year) was owned by employees, with a
market value exceeding $750 billion. Gates notes, further, that
about a dozen publicly traded companies are now majority em-
ployee-owned, including United Airlines (with 85,000 employees),
Science Applications International Corporation, and Amsted
Industries. Well-known companies with at least 30 percent employee ownership include Northwest Airlines, Tandy Corporation, and Hallmark Cards, Inc. More and more companies are
making stock options broadly available to employees. A 1997

study by William M. Mercer Consultants, which Gates mentions, found that 30 percent of larger American companies now have such broad-based plans covering more than half their employees, up from 17 percent in 1992.[57]

Despite the increase in popularity and participation of ESOPs, they are no magic bullet for a company's problems according to Jeff Gates.

> Employee ownership is not without its risks. While detractors worry that "all their eggs are in one basket," supporters worry that employees frequently have neither eggs nor a basket. There is little that employee ownership alone can do to insulate companies from competition, technological change, or shifting markets. Nor is there anything "magical" about employees owning shares if the company is in the wrong business. On the other hand, some companies embrace employee ownership as a component of their competitiveness strategy, figuring that at-risk employee owners are more likely to exhibit the entrepreneurial drive and flexibility required to identify and make the changes required as technology changes and markets shift.[58]

Despite Gates' cautionary note, he also reports some stunning success stories in employee ownership, most notably Science Applications International Corporation (SAIC) of San Diego. Bob Beyster, the founder and CEO of SAIC, believes that employee ownership has been a key to the firm's success throughout the 1990s in identifying new opportunities, even as it began to lose its largest customer, the Department of Defense, to ongoing budget cuts.

> With its eclectic mix of a dozen different employee stock plans, including stock grants for employees who bring in new business, and for those identified as future leaders, SAIC has almost tripled its workforce since the early 1990s, while cutbacks have been the hallmark of most defense firms. Success, they found, was not just about market share; it was also about creating new markets—

markets that at-risk, motivated employees proved adept at creating. *Inc.* magazine, in whose pages employee ownership is often extolled, reports "there's considerable evidence that eliminating the employee mentality and creating companies of business people, of owners, has become a kind of Hidden Secret of Success in the American marketplace. That's certainly the case at SAIC where, as *Forbes* reports, CEO Beyster, with his spread-the-wealth management, "doesn't have to worry about what Wall Street analysts think of his company. His bosses work for him."[59]

The question might be fairly asked whether or not SAIC is an isolated example of success, or whether companies with a significant degree of employee ownership outperform companies without ESOPs. In a short piece in *Time* magazine, Daniel Eisenberg reports that companies with ESOPs handily outperform companies without, using total return to shareholders as a measure of performance.[60] In a study carried out by Hewitt Associates, firms with ESOPs enjoyed an advantage in total shareholder return of 26 to 19 percent. While the Hewitt study did not attempt to measure the entire stream of values of the companies in question, it is a good bet that the outstanding performance of the firms with ESOPs was more than just financial. Broadening the ownership base of more and more organizations may well prove to be a powerful means of creating value in American society, and around the world.

Value Driver 8: Competitor Values

> ''This industry is always in the grip of its dumbest competitors.''—Robert Crandall, Chairman and CEO of American Airlines, in an interview with Janice Castro of *Time* Magazine, May 4, 1992.

As a group, the executives of America's airlines love to buy planes. The newer jets, like Boeing's 757, are significantly more fuel efficient than older planes like Boeing's venerable 707; since jet fuel is a major cost factor in the industry, efficiency is a major reason the newer aircraft are attractive to the airlines. When a major airline is faced with traffic growth, and growth has been fairly steady since the 1950s, its executives generally place orders for new planes. This would seem to be sensible and logical executive behavior, on the face of it, but the nature of the industry—and its competitive values—can create major financial problems for most carriers.

Writing on this topic in the *Denver Times* late in 1995, syndicated columnist Adam Bryant of *The New York Times* warned long-term investors to stay away from airline stocks.

> Since 1958, for example, airlines have developed a predictable pattern in buying planes. Faced with strong traffic growth, they typically order a large number of aircraft. But because the planes cannot be delivered for a few years, traffic growth often trails off as the new planes hit the market. That leaves the industry with too many airline seats chasing too few customers. Fare wars then flare up as the airlines try to fill the empty seats. That, combined with external shocks like the Persian Gulf war (note: during which airline traffic declined dramatically), has led to billions of dollars in carrier losses.[61]

Columnist Bryant also notes that airlines face many pressures to grow. Their leaders fear losing market share as air traffic increases, and so they almost compulsively buy new aircraft, aided by enthusiastic bankers who view the airlines as cash cows that will reliably make payments on their loans.

During an economic downturn (such as the one that occurred after the 1991 Persian Gulf war), however, cash cows suddenly lose their supply of milk. A downturn in revenues leaves all the major carriers financially strapped since none of them have significant reserves after using all their money to buy new aircraft. The ensuing panic may set off a ruinous price war, such as the one that occurred in 1992 that led to the dramatic statement by American CEO Robert Crandall that introduces this section. In the same interview he was asked by Janice Castro of *Time* how long it would be before air fares would stabilize after Carl

Icahn—the former CEO of hapless TWA—set off a new fare war with a series of cuts in prices. Crandall's reply has become a classic:

> I simply don't know. This industry is always in the grip of its dumbest competitors. I was surprised when TWA cut fares. I don't understand TWA's strategy. It doesn't make any sense, and therefore I don't know what they will do to further lower fares. All I know is that we have no choice but to match whatever low fare anybody puts out there. And so it will get as bad as they want it to get.[62]

The futility and the destruction of value for all competitors of a fare war are expressed in this eloquent statement. Such wars erupt, as Adam Bryant noted, during a cash crunch when empty seats need to be filled; and it is usually one of the most strapped competitors who will set it off, normally in the hope that the discounted fares will provide a fast cash injection to get the airline over the hump. Gary Gardiner commented on this phenomenon in *21st Century Manager*:

> The general impact of severe financial losses (such as the airline industry was experiencing in the early 1990s) is to force an organization, or an entire industry, into a self-defeating reactive or overreactive pattern, which usually involves not only questionable business practices but also a good deal of MBCCP (Management by Crisis, Chaos, and Panic): hasty, desperate, and poorly considered strategic moves are made that further weaken the company. Currently the airline industry, which does not seem to learn from its mistakes and has a long history of cash-flow woes, continues to engage in an annual round of ticket-discounting that in the short-run may pump up earnings for the first carrier that announces its air-fare sale but in the long run damages the whole industry. The short-term self-interest of one carrier hurts the interests of all.[63]

The behavior and values of one competitor often influence the behavior of others, and we see this carried to an extreme in the airline industry when a fare war breaks out. In the late 1990s, despite an occasional round of price cutting, a truly destructive war has not developed, perhaps because of the improved financial health of most carriers in a robust economy, or perhaps because they have learned not to let their strategy be dictated by the dumbest competitor. Watch their behavior, however, during the next economic downturn.

If the airline industry represents the worst of short-term thinking and the destructive impact of competitors' behavior, an emerging industry—the world of Internet commerce—may well demonstrate the power of strategic, proactive, and Value Driven Management, and the positive impact of competitors' values.

The phenomenal growth of Internet—or "Net"—companies in the mid- to late 1990s has been well documented, as has the fact that many of them have never made a nickel, at least at the time of this writing. Despite their current lack of profitability, Net companies like Amazon.com have stock values and market capitalization that are totally unprecedented. When founder and CEO Jeff Bezos opened what Amazon.com likes to call its virtual doors in July 1995, the company was simply an online bookseller that did not warehouse a single volume, since it had no warehouse. All sales were handled by a major book wholesaler, Ingram, and the company simply processed orders. Despite the fact that it had never been profitable, Bezos took his company public in May 1997 with an IPO (Initial Public Offering) of $3 per share.

The rest, as the saying goes, is history. By spring of 1999, Amazon's stock was trading in the $175-a-share range, and its total market capitalization was close to $29 billion. The company was now far more than just a bookseller, as hedge fund manager and author James J. Cramer pointed out in a short article in *Time* magazine entitled "Long-Term Carping."

> Amazon, once criticized as a bookseller that would never show a profit, turns out to have used its online book business as a template for forays into music, drugs, pets, and this week, online auctions, perhaps the hottest area on the Web. Maybe its $28 billion market cap isn't so wacky if Amazon becomes the world's first online department store.[64]

Cramer's article notes that for years American executives and managers have been blamed for short-term thinking, ". . . cowed by Wall Street—the nerve!—to make the quarterly number or see their stock price sacrificed to the earnings gods."[65] He views the new generation of CEOs of online firms—like Jeff Bezos, Tim Koogle of Yahoo, Steve Case of America Online, and Tom Jermoluk of @Home—as a new breed of manager, leaders who think long term, who pursue aggressive acquisition strategies, and who are not a bit worried by a lack of short-term profitability. "These young chieftains have shown a true disdain for the next quarter's results. In fact, Amazon's Bezos went so far as to urge those concerned with short-term performance to *sell* his stock, something no one else has ever done in the 20 years I have been trading."[66]

Cramer debunks the prevailing notion that Internet businesses are worthless until they become profitable, pointing out that companies like Amazon (which has experienced phenomenal sales growth) are building brands that could be worth many times more than their current prices. He also recognizes, however, that some of the e-companies will inevitably go under, which will wipe out previously unheard amounts of shareholder value. This new generation of executives, he says, ". . . is managing for a world that doesn't even exist and may not for years, a world of thousands of intertwined communities in constant contact over the Internet."[67] From the point of view of Value Driven Management, these executives share positive and proactive competitive values. They are risk takers who think long term, who will develop industries that no one has yet thought of, and who create value in ways that will truly dazzle business analysts and academicians. It is not likely, however, that they will engage in foolish price wars that will destroy value for their companies and the brave new world of Internet commerce.

The Fit, the Futile, and the Failed: Value Gained and Value Lost

Without exception, the companies who have survived crises, and even thrived on them, have been proactive, strategic firms that have made decisions under pressure that took into account the full complexity of the problems before them. They refused to bow to short-term pressures, kept their heads, and did their best to think things through. Often they were fortunate enough to have enlightened and wise CEOs at the helm, but they were also equally fortunate to have hundreds of bright men and women working for them. Many times these men and women enjoyed active and broad ownership rights in the company. Without exception, they used a multidimensional and value-driven process in making the decisions they did. These are the truly fit, fine, and competitive companies, and they are to be admired (with reservations, of course) because the sometimes stern discipline of the marketplace can humble the finest organization, and in a hurry, if it ceases to be ever alert, anticipatory, and vigilant.

On the other hand, the companies we have described who have failed to cope effectively with the problems they found themselves facing, and who in many cases turned them into true crises, often made hasty and ill-considered decisions that made things worse. They often overreacted to, or simply failed to consider, important dimensions of the situation: value drivers that should have been important in their decision-making process were overlooked, discounted, or never considered. Such organizations must surely live with a sense of futility, or even with a sense of impending doom. Value Driven Management, when it is practiced faithfully and fully, can break the back of the psychology of overreaction and failure, and provide organizations with a powerful decision-making process that will create value over time.

Endnotes

1. Michael Schachner, "Exxon a Victim of Its Attitude: Lawyer," *Business Insurance* 29 (February 1995): 4.
2. Ibid., 4–5.
3. "Another Hash at Denny's; Discrimination Cases in 1994 Might Not Have Delivered the Lesson," *The Los Angeles Times*, 31 August 1997, sec. M, p. 4.
4. "Denny's Apologizes in Discrimination Complaint," *Florida Times Union*, 6 May 1998, sec. B, p. 4.

5. Bruce Smith, "Denny's Ads Sell Diversity: Chain to Spend $2 Million on Commercials as Part of Settlement in Discrimination Suit," *Detroit News*, 13 January 1999, sec. B, p. 3.
6. Richard T. De George, *Business Ethics*, 4th ed. (Englewood Cliffs, NJ: Prentice Hall, 1995), 3–4.
7. Ibid., 3–4.
8. William May, "Good Ethics Is Good Business," *New Management*, Spring 1987, 56–61.
9. Ibid., 59.
10. Lou Dobbs, "Market-Based Management—Koch Industries," *Management with Lou Dobbs*, CNN News, 14 October 1995.
11. Charles Koch, as quoted in Wayne Gable and Jerry Ellig, *Introduction to Market-Based Management* (Fairfax, VA: Center for Market Processes, 1933), 2–3.
12. Ibid., 3.
13. Annual Report, Koch Industries, Inc., Wichita, Kansas, 1999. Reprinted with permission.
14. Ibid.
15. Ibid.
16. Allanna Sullivan and Peter Fritsch, "Texaco Punishes Officials Over Racist Epithets," *The Wall Street Journal*, 11 November 1996, sec. A, p. 2.
17. Adam Bryant, "How Much Has Texaco Changed?" *New York Times*, 2 November 1997.
18. Raymond A. Noe, John R. Hollenbeck, Barry Gerhart, and Patrick M. Wright, *Human Resource Management*, 2nd ed. (New York: McGraw-Hill, 1996), 158–159.
19. Stephanie Gruner, "Have Fun, Make Money," *Inc.*, May 1998, 123.
20. Daniel Pederson, "Wal-Mart of the Sky," *Newsweek*, 1 March 1999, 47.
21. Michael Porter, "What Is Strategy?" *Harvard Business Review*, November-December 1996, 61–78.
22. Noe et al., *Human Resource Management*, 327.
23. Robert C. Preziosi, "The Impact of Value-Based Leadership on Organizational Productivity," in *Productivity and Quality Management Frontiers*, Vol. 6, ed. Carl G. Thor, Johnson A. Edosomwan, Robert Poupart, and David J. Sumanth (Norcross, GA: Engineering and Management Press, 1997), 12–18.
24. Robert C. Preziosi and Pedro F. Pellet, "The Relationship Between Value Consistency and Productivity," *Productivity and Quality Management Frontiers*, Vol. 7, ed. David J. Sumanth, William B. Werther, Jr. and Johnson A. Edosomwan, (Norcross, GA: Engineering and Management Press, 1998), 299–302.

25. William J. Harrington, Robert C. Preziosi, and Jean Gordon, "Nurses' Perception of the Relationship Between Values Consistency and Total Quality in a Public Hospital" (paper presented at the *International Conference on Productivity and Quality Research*, 1999).

26. Jean Gordon, "The Relationship Between the Critical-Care Nurses/ Hospital Management, and Perceived Total Quality Management Practices in a South Florida Public Hospital" (DBA diss. Nova Southeastern University, 1999).

27. Nathaniel Branden, *Taking Responsibility* (New York: Simon & Schuster, 1996), 12.

28. O. C. Ferrell and Gareth S. Gardiner, *In Pursuit of Ethics* (Springfield, IL: Smith Collins, 1991).

29. W. Alan Randolph, "Navigating the Journey to Empowerment," *Organizational Dynamics*, Spring 1995, 22.

30. Thomas J. Peters and Robert H. Waterman, Jr., *In Search of Excellence: Lessons from America's Best-Run Companies* (New York: Harper & Row, 1982).

31. O. C. Ferrell and Geoffrey Hirt, *Business: A Changing World* (Boston: Houghton Mifflin, 1996), 321.

32. Art Weinstein and Randolph A. Pohlman, "Customer Value: A New Paradigm for Marketing Management," *Advances in Business Studies* 6, no. 10 (1998): 90.

33. Ibid., 91.

34. Ibid., 92.

35. Ibid., 93.

36. Art Weinstein and William C. Johnson, *Designing and Delivering Superior Customer Value: Concepts, Cases, and Applications* (Boca Raton, FL: CRC/St. Lucie Press, 1999).

37. Robert Spector and Patrick D. McCarthy, *The Nordstrom Way* (Chicago: Audio-Tech Business Book Summaries, 1995), 2.

38. Ibid., 3–4.

39. Ibid., 6–7.

40. John T. Landry, "Supply Chain Management: The Case for Alliances," *Harvard Business Review*, November-December 1998, 24–25.

41. Ibid.

42. Ibid., 25.

43. Kathleen Kerwin, "GM: Modular Plants Won't Be a Snap," *Business Week*, 9 November 1998, 168.

44. Ibid., 172.

45. Ibid.

46. George Will, "The Trouble with Modern-Day Baseball," New Orleans *Times-Picayune*, 1 March 1999, sec. B, p. 5.

47. Richard J. Mahoney, "Business Should Act for All Its Stakeholders—before 'The Feds' Do," *The CEO Series*, no. 9 (St. Louis, MO: Center for the Study of American Business, 1996).
48. Ibid., 2–3.
49. Ibid., 4.
50. Roberto C. Goizueta, "Why Shareowner Value?" *The CEO Series*, no. 13 (St. Louis, MO: Center for the Study of American Business, 1997), 4–5.
51. "Coca-Cola CEO Dies at 65," *Corporate Observer*, Spring 1998, 1.
52. Richard J. Mahoney, "The Shareowner's Voice: Are We 'Listening to Prozac'?" *The CEO Series*, no. 17 (St. Louis, MO: Center for the Study of American Business, 1997), 1.
53. Ibid., 4.
54. Ibid., 5.
55. Goizueta, "Why Shareowner Value?" 4–5.
56. Jeffrey R. Gates, *The Ownership Solution* (Reading, MA: Addison-Wesley, 1998), 60.
57. Ibid., 61.
58. Ibid., 62.
59. Ibid.
60. Daniel Eisenberg, "No ESOP Fable," *Time*, 10 May 1999, 95.
61. Adam Bryant, "Airline Investors May Find Long Rides Turbulent," *Denver Post*, 10 December 1995, sec. G, p. 3.
62. Janice Castro, "This Industry Is Always in the Grip of Its Dumbest Competitors," *Time*, 4 May 1992, 52.
63. Gareth S. Gardiner, *21st Century Manager* (Princeton, NJ: Peterson's/Pacesetter Books, 1996).
64. James J. Cramer, "Long-Term Carping," *Time*, 12 April 1999, 101.
65. Ibid.
66. Ibid.
67. Ibid.

Part III

Implementing Value Driven Management

Chapter 6

The Balancing Act: Making Value Driven Management Work in Your Organization

In order to maximize value over time, eight value drivers must be juggled and balanced. Such decision making is always complex, sometimes intuitive, and usually subject to some degree of pressure or stress. The organizations that do best in difficult situations are almost always those who continue to process complex information in a clear way, who keep their cool when others lose their heads—and not because they do not understand the problem—and who continue to be cognizant of constituent values. Implementing Value Driven Management in organizations is a seven-step process involving commitment and support from the top down, developing a more open and participative organization, restructuring compensation and the entire organization to support the creation of value, careful selection of employees, and making value creation the topic of the day—everyday. Organization-wide training in balancing and juggling the eight value drivers in the decision-making process is perhaps the most vital necessity in the implementation process, along with the recognition that ongoing and lifelong education is simply a fact of life in the successful and value-driven organization.

Most of us feel "normal" the majority of time. Despite bad jokes about what and who is or is not normal, most of us know what it means to feel normal. Generally we feel O.K.; we feel clear-headed; we do not feel the need to rush frantically from place to place; we enjoy positive relationships with our friends and colleagues; and generally we have a pretty decent quality of life. Life changes, however, when a crisis erupts. It may be an unexpected illness or death in the family, an unexpected job layoff or termination, or a traumatic and totally unanticipated financial emergency. Admittedly, the first two events often lead to the third, particularly in contemporary American society. In such life changes, our anxiety level can reach near panic, we may feel confused and indecisive, and we may suffer from unexpected physical problems—skin rashes, diarrhea, headaches, sleeplessness, and other undignified symptoms—and we become irritable, impatient, and difficult to be around. Our quality of life goes down the drain; metaphorically speaking.

Individuals who are familiar with these symptoms never forget the stressful and traumatic episodes in their lives. Often what comes out of such episodes, however, is a personal triumph: We cope with the unpleasant symptoms, we make sensible and intelligent decisions that get us through the crisis, and we become stronger people as a result, thus affirming the wisdom of a popular saying in the field of psychology: Any experience we have in this lifetime that does not kill or maim us makes us stronger—particularly if we have the wisdom to learn from it. However, this does not make extreme stress, as compared to the normal aggravations of a middle-class professional life in contemporary America, any more pleasant to deal with.

What is the relevance of all this to Value Driven Management? The answer lies in how individuals and organizations conduct themselves in good times and bad. How they make decisions and take actions reveals a great deal about how they *really* function and what they *really* value. In particular, when companies like Johnson & Johnson or Exxon go through a major crisis, we learn a great deal about their true character, and how they juggle and balance values as they cope with an unanticipated problem or crisis. It is also quite possible that these firms learn things about themselves, and that their true colors come shining through, or do not shine through, as the case may be.

Information Processing and Decision Making, in Good Times and Bad

Some 35 years ago, at the very dawning of the information age, researchers in the field of organizational and social psychology at Princeton University, and other centers of higher learning throughout the country, began to investigate the manner in which individuals and organizations process information—how they use information in their thinking and decision making, and how information processing differs in different settings—on the assumption that there would be important, and even critical, differences among people and the firms they worked for in how effective their information processes were. This assumption turned out to be a sound one, and hundreds of studies carried out in the four decades since the 1960s have corroborated early findings that there are indeed very important differences in individual and organizational information-processing styles, and that these differences are important to both individual and organizational success.

The early findings that came out of the social psychology laboratory at Princeton, which we referred to briefly in Chapter 4 (and where Gary Gardiner was heavily involved in the research program on the nature of what has come to be called *conceptual complexity*), set the tone for the field.[1] The Princeton research program initially focused on individual differences in information processing, and early work showed that some individuals are superior in the way they use information: individuals high in cognitive or conceptual complexity typically use *more* information in their problem-solving and decision-making processes and generate *more and better alternative solutions* to problems than persons lower in complexity.

The personality correlates of conceptual complexity are also fascinating. Persons higher in complexity are often more creative, less prejudiced, less prone to make snap judgements, more tolerant of ambiguity, more disciplined, less rigid and dogmatic, and more democratic in personality structure than persons lower in complexity. Persons high in complexity consistently came from homes and educational institutions that valued independent thinking, encouraged students to think for themselves, and placed minimal or no emphasis on *rote learning*: memorization, regurgitation, and dutiful copying down of the instructor's dog-eared lecture notes—what some contemporary educators con-temptuously call the "scarf and barf" model.

Like individuals, organizations differ consistently and dra-matically in the way they process information and make deci-sions. Organizations that are run from the top-down by an autocratic CEO may sometimes be brilliantly successful in the short-run, if the dictator is smart, but their simplistic or impul-sive decision making will consistently lead them into trouble: They will often overreact and self-destruct when faced with a pe-riod of stress and turbulence. Firms that are more participative and make good use of valuable human assets, on the other hand, process information in a much more complex way than authori-tarian companies, and are likely to do better when the time inevi-tably comes to weather a downturn in the business cycle or deal with a major crisis. The pages of this book are already filled with negative and positive examples of firms in crisis.

Periods of stress or crisis are not only difficult for any person or company to cope with, they have the general effect of *lowering the complexity of information processing*: people and organiza-tions tend to regress somewhat under duress, using less informa-tion and making hastier judgments, but the more sophisticated ones—in terms of information processing—hold up better.

Nordstrom Revisited: A Good Company in the Midst of Stress

We are a society that often holds up successful athletes as role models for our young people. This is a process that involves haz-ards, since some well-known athletes run amok—alcohol, drugs, violence, and sex are the usual culprits. When such a role model strays seriously, we need to do some revisionist thinking and quickly, before we move on to the next choice. We are being a bit cynical, of course, but we business authors also run a serious risk when we hold up a single company as a role model for all good businesspersons to follow: Even our most distinguished corporations can also run amok, particularly in a customer-driven, rapidly-changing, globalized economy, and they can do so quickly. It is with this realistic consideration in mind that we return to a company that we have praised mightily in these pages: Nordstrom.

Unexpectedly, late in the 1990s, Nordstrom experienced a period of intense stress, precipitated by the usual villains in the business world: customer defections resulting in slowing sales, weak earnings, erratic stock performance, and some previously undiagnosed—but very real—organizational problems. As Seanna Browder of *Business Week* comments in an article tellingly entitled "Great Service Wasn't Enough," Nordstrom ran into serious problems after it launched an aggressive expansion strategy.

> It looked like a slam-dunk. In the late 1980s, Seattle-based Nordstrom Inc. set the gold standard in department-store retailing. Its reputation for quality, fashion, and customer care was unparalleled, its customers among the most loyal in the industry. And while other chains were still reeling from the buyout craze of the decade, Nordstrom profits were growing by double digits. So the decision to expand beyond the West Coast seemed like a no-brainer.[2]

Things did not work out quite that way, however, as columnist Browder notes.

The underlying problem was apparently a growth strategy that had not been fully thought through: Important value drivers had not been juggled and balanced, nor perhaps even taken into consideration. Interestingly, the company's organizational culture, which had served it so well when it was just a regional chain, became a serious stumbling block when Nordstrom decided to go national. The firm had long used a totally noncomputerized and "quaint"[3] system of handwritten notes kept by associates on customer preferences. These had worked well previously, but were totally inadequate after expansion, causing the company to lose track of changes in fashion trends—the same illness that afflicted Levi Strauss when teen-aged buyers of blue jeans turned away from its traditionally successful brands and styles. In market-based management and Value Driven Management, anticipating changes in customer demands, which can be fickle, complex, and volatile, is one of the most difficult and stressful challenges any company can face, particularly in the garment industry.

In addition to the totally swamped system of manual tracking, Nordstrom failed to centralize common functions such as buying. Its system of decentralized buying (*Business Week's* Browder points out that it had 900 buyers chain-wide, when competitor R. H. Macy & Co. had only 100) drove vendors crazy because it resulted in a blizzard of conflicting or duplicative orders. The marketing effort was also fragmented because its ads were created regionally by in-house teams. Earnings and the company's share price (it is publicly traded on the New York Stock Exchange) began to suffer: Net income in 1996 dropped 11 percent to $147 million, and the share price—which had been as high as $53 in 1996—dropped as low as $34 in 1997 before it recovered somewhat, and late in 1999 was trading in the $30 to $40 range.

Financial damage resulting from a failed strategic initiative may be relative, and Nordstrom has very deep pockets, but the company was under intense pressure not only from industry analysts, but from its other constituents to take action to do something to keep customers from continuing to bail out. And there was no question they were doing just that. Nordstrom had missed some major emerging trends in women's fashions, such as a switch to more casual styles suitable for today's more informal work environments. It continued to rely on more formal, buttoned-down garments, and customers were turned off and began shopping elsewhere.

In the short-term, perhaps predictably, Nordstrom did what most firms, including world-class ones do in a crunch: it cut costs. The number of buyers was reduced by nearly 20 percent, the company was organized into divisions, and inventory was cut dramatically; all of which resulted in a jump in net income to $207 million for the fiscal year ending in January 1999. This move was an obvious attempt to appease investors and analysts.

Long-term, however, strategic changes also needed to be

made, and some important changes *have* been made. A brand new multimillion-dollar data center has been built in Denver to handle basic and vital information-processing tasks, such as developing a database on buying habits and trends and using the new computers to manage inventory more efficiently. Nordstrom is the last of the major retailers to computerize operations management, and *Business Week* comments that even the salespeople's handwritten notes that had historically been placed in binders are now going online.[4] The company has also made a move into Internet retailing, although its e-commerce Web site is not yet profitable. The goal of all this activity, of course, is increased profitability: to install a more attractive and fashionable merchandise mix that will bring customers back into the stores, and to increase same-store sales, which had dropped by over 2½ percent per store during the company's slump.

Perhaps most interesting, however, is the fact that Nordstrom's Office of the President, which currently consists of six brothers and cousins who hold the title of Co-President (the largest and most unusual chief executive officer group in American industry, and perhaps in American history), is being restructured. Several new outside executives have been brought in to incorporate a new perspective into the firm's decision-making process. In addition to this important move, the company also hired a consulting firm (Marakon Associates, Stamford, Connecticut) to assist Nordstrom in its strategic-management process. Marakon has already recommended that the company create more clearly defined areas of responsibility for the six co-CEOs, so that they work more effectively together as a team, and make better decisions—as well as not getting in each other's way. Marakon's managing partner, Paul Favaro, believes that the firm's unorthodox management structure can be a strength, not a liability, if the six relatives learn to work together and make clear and effective decisions.[5]

From the point of view of managing stress, and processing information more effectively, it appears that Nordstrom is on the right track. During its expansionary growing pains, and accompanying sales slump, its cost-cutting measures were undoubtedly necessary to stabilize the firm in the short-run, and prevent a wholesale sell-off of its stock. This is hardly a wildly overreactive and panicky reaction to a real problem, particularly since long-term and strategic moves—like the development of its computer center in Denver—were also being made that are almost certain to create value for Nordstrom in the future. While a history of success and a reputation for being a world-class company are no guarantee of continued success, such companies (IBM and Levi Strauss are two that rapidly come to mind) seem to come through periods of strain and stress successfully, emerging as even stronger corporate entities. From our point of view, this is in large part because they have never lost sight of the fact that their mission is to create value for all their constituents over the long run, which gives them an inner resilience and ability to persevere that not all firms share. The authors are reminded, again, of the wise words of the late Roberto C. Goizueta of the Coca-Cola Company, "To make yourself of unique value to your share owners over the long haul, you must also make yourself of unique value to your consumers, customers, partners, and fellow employees *over the long haul.*"[6]

Implementing Value Driven Management

Value Driven Management is no quick fix, flavor-of-the month, management bandwagon, nor a consultant's magic wand. The history of management, as we have already noted, is full of such management fads that have come and gone. Often a CEO, desperate to turn around a troubled organization, will latch on to such an instant solution for his or her firm's troubles. The quick fix inevitably becomes part of the problem, however, or actually makes it worse because the organization's employees become understandably cynical and mistrustful, and the new management miracle is never given a fair chance. Value Driven Management is no miracle cure, and it requires a sustained commitment and a fairly lengthy period of organizational development.

The authors believe, based on years of executive and consulting experience, that the process of integrating Value Driven Management into an organization's culture requires a minimum time frame of three years, and in some settings may require more. Koch Industries, for example, has been evolving a market-based and value-driven culture for more than 30 years. It is now three decades plus since Charles Koch became CEO in 1967, and Randy Pohlman recalls his statements on numerous occasions that the process of implementing such a culture is still far from finished. Koch is unique, of course, in that it has had stable, continuing, and in our opinion, value-based, leadership for such a long period of time. Heaven help the company that replaces its CEO every one or two years, because this is exactly the firm that will be looking for a management miracle to bail it out.

When Gary Gardiner was recently doing a training program at Boeing's St. Louis operation, his most vivid memory of the experience was a large and artistic chart that had been placed on the wall just outside the training room. Its four- to five-foot length contained a graphic and humorous history of every management movement the company had been through over a 25-year period (encompassing both its corporate history as McDonnell-Douglas and Boeing), including Total Quality Management, Management by Objectives, quality circles, process improvement, and at least a dozen other such programs or fads. The participants in the program took great pleasure in looking at the chart during breaks and made all kinds of humorous remarks about its contents.

Beneath their good humor, however, one could sense a real feeling of tiredness and disillusionment: They had truly seen it all. Despite the fact that the people involved in the program were bright, competent, and decent human beings; doing management training in such an environment is a challenge. Understandably, the group wondered what tricks in his kit bag *this* particular consultant had to offer; and Gardiner had to somewhat apologetically acknowledge that he was just an old dog with no new tricks in his bag.

Implementing Value Driven Management does not require a bag of tricks, nor managerial sleight of hand, but it *does* require commitment from the organization's leadership, accompanied by the recognition that the company is in it for the long haul. In fact, it is a process that is never done.

Step 1: Management Commitment

Step 1 in creating a Value Driven Culture, and probably the most critical, is *long-term commitment from top management to its im-*

plementation throughout the organization, accompanied by a commitment to communicate its importance to the organization, the industry or industries it finds itself in, and to all its constituents. The process of communication and commitment has as its goal what we like to call a VMPP: an intensive process of creating a shared Vision, Mission, organizational Philosophy, and business Principles that support and facilitate the development of a Value Driven Culture.

Our managerial acronyms may not be as nifty and catchy as MBO or TQM but it is our strong feeling that *they do not have to be*: When employees throughout the organization—and every person in the organization is an employee—understand the importance and value of the philosophy of Value Driven Management, an important first step toward implementation will have begun.

At some point in the process, the VMPP *must be written down*. Koch Industries had been involved in the value creation process for many years before the marvelous statements of mission, philosophy, and business practices (principles) that appear in Chapter 5 were actually reduced to writing. Prior to that time, they were well understood because they had been communicated verbally, through actions, and repeatedly to everyone in the firm, but the process of formalizing them in clear and value driven written statements greatly helped further the process. This process becomes ever more important as the organization experiences *growth*. When firms are small, they are in many ways like a family, with close and informal relationships present among many of the members, but as they become larger, and must hire and assimilate new members, the written VMPP becomes an important guide to action, and can be built right into the hiring process itself.

In a very real way, therefore, *the commitment process begins at the top, but it must not end there.* If Value Driven Management is perceived as just a new management fad brought home from a conference by the firm's latest CEO, it will surely have no better fate than the two, or three, or twelve management fads that have preceded it—perfectly suitable for a five-foot long chart on the corporate wall, and subject to hoots and hollers from employees who now await the *next* fad the *next* CEO will bring home.

Step 1 and the other six steps involved in implementing Value Driven Management are summarized in Figure 6-1.

Step 2: Employee Empowerment

Step 2 is another logical and positive step that flows logically from Step 1. *Every employee must not only be an employee, but must also be an empowered employee.* Decision-making rights, and the right to take risks, must not only be spread to every person in the organization, but they must *saturate* the firm. In today's globalized, high-technology economy organizations that are run from the top down, that are authoritarian and/or abusive, and that do not invest significant resources in retaining and developing their human assets, will simply not survive.

Many organizations continue to give lip service to empowerment, just as they do to the principle of putting the customer first, but when their management and decision-making practices are analyzed, they are really just traditional and bureaucratized firms; or worse, they make hasty and ill-considered strategic moves under stress, which usually involve massive layoffs and other cost-cutting moves that demoralize almost everyone in the organization, and fail to produce value-creating initiatives that will see the organization through in the long-term.

Organizations that are genuinely *value driven,* and that also make at least some use of fully empowered and *self-directed work teams,* are usually more productive—particularly over time—than organizations that are exploitative and authoritarian. Rensis Likert, the director of the Institute for Social Research at the University of Michigan, and whose work was already mentioned in Chapter 4, began studying this organizational phenomenon over 35 years ago. His research has shown again and again that participative organizations outperform nonparticipative ones. In two classic volumes, *New Patterns of Management* and *The Human Organization,* he reported research that demonstrated this fact, but he also showed that *time* is a critical variable in developing organizations.[7, 8] When an organization seeks to create value by empowering its employees, and by building its human asset base through using participative management, and when it tries hard to lead, live, and reinforce its values, productivity may actually

Figure 6-1   The seven critical steps in implementing value driven management.

Step 1—*A long-term commitment from top management to its implementation throughout the organization.* No quick fixes, magic bullets, or flavor of the month, but a sober recognition that successfully implementing Value Driven Management may require a minimum of three years, and is an ongoing, lifelong commitment.

Step 2—*Every employee must not only be an employee, but must also be an empowered employee.* The organization must be open and participative so that it can create knowledge.

Step 3—*Compensation must be tied to value-creating behavior in every unit and at every level throughout the organization.* Compensation schemes such as profit sharing, employee stock ownership, gainsharing, and team or group bonuses, will stimulate long-term productivity and value creation.

Step 4—*The organization must be restructured as needed to facilitate value creation.* The traditional, hierarchical organization is not well suited to creating value in the complex global economy, but flatter, team- and work-process oriented firms do much better.

Step 5—*There must be systematic and organization-wide selection of employees who will create value in the positions they fill.* Southwest Airlines, for example, seeks out employees who can think for themselves, and use their own judgment.

Step 6—*Value creation must be the topic of the day, every day.* Spontaneous celebrations of excellence, and other forms of reaffirmation, will continuously revitalize a value-driven organizational culture. Every employee must be committed to value creation every day.

Step 7—*There must be ongoing, comprehensive, and lifelong education of all the employees of the organization in the balancing act: How to use Value Driven Management in the organizational decision-making process.* Comprehensive training will eventually produce an organization whose members are both consciously and unconsciously competent, and who can use a complex information-processing set of techniques to systematically create value.

decrease in the short run. This is one of the ironies revealed by Likert's research, along with the fact that in the short run what Gary Gardiner calls "tough-guy" management (Theory "X," authoritarian, overreactive, and exploitative) may even *increase* productivity. Management by fear, which is the emotion that this type of management depends on, may produce positive short-term results because human beings respond immediately to fear. Punishment works in the short run because it motivates people to avoid the punishment; in the long run it is counterproductive, because it loses its power.[9]

Management that builds upon higher-level needs, however, can take a significant amount of time to be effective. Employees are often mistrustful and fearful of the change, not only because they have never seen a more positive management system at work, but because they fear that it will not last—and that it will simply saddle them with additional responsibilities and no additional compensation. Likert estimates that what he calls System 4 management—participative/group management—can take at least a year to begin showing results, and that in the short run (three to six months), it may lead to decreased productivity, even in the most skilled hands, as the human beings in the organization begin to adjust to the change.

As the change to System 4 takes place, good things begin to happen. Employees become more empowered, and the entire organization begins to become more proactive, particularly as its members take on more and more responsibility for its success—and their own. Value Driven Management requires open and free information sharing to be effective, and this process of openness begins to create knowledge throughout the organization. As the human asset base and the firm become more and more knowledgeable and skilled, and become more and more capable of complex information processing and decision making, they and it become more and more able to *anticipate* changing customer desires, and other important changes in the global marketplace, including technology, economic conditions, and even cultural and working conditions.

As we have previously pointed out, one of the inevitable consequences of authoritarian management or nonvalue driven management and command economies, is the lack of, or drying up of, information that is absolutely vital to organizational success. Very simplistic information processing and decision making is virtually guaranteed in such environments. Participative, open and value-driven firms, on the other hand, are well suited to the openness and complexity of market economies because they constantly create information and develop knowledge that creates value for the organization.

One of the techniques that value-driven firms can use to empower their employees and to open up the organization, is to make sure that employees have all the information they need to make good decisions about their jobs and problems that may go far beyond their immediate job responsibilities.

Step 3: Compensation

Step 3 is every bit as critical in the implementation process as Step 2, and that is the necessity to *tie compensation to value-creating behavior in every unit and at every level throughout the organization*. People respond to incentives, Steven Landsburg said, and the rest is pretty much commentary. Compensation is not the only incentive that exists in a firm, of course. For many employees, however, compensation is one of the most powerful incentives in their work lives, although there is increasing evidence that this historical fact is changing, particularly among professionals and skilled workers in high-tech industries, where other needs are becoming more paramount. How an organization handles compensation, however, and how it structures pay, can be a powerful force in creating value, or it can become a major impediment to the implementation of Value Driven Management.

Historically, firms were organized on the one-man/one-boss principle, at a time when most companies were still tall, vertical, and strictly hierarchical, and when women and members of minority groups had not become a major force in the workplace. In such an organizational milieu, pay was administered through the hierarchy. Pay grades and ranges for different jobs in the organizations were largely established from the top down, with little or no input from front-line management or lower-level employees, and pay raises were determined by management and handed down annually to grateful employees. Millions and millions of working and retired Americans remember the system well: All too often raise time meant going to the boss, cap in hand, to virtually beg for a pay increase—a demeaning psychology at best. The system was not intended to work this way, of course, since virtually every system stated that performance, skill, and productivity were to be the bases for raises. But with the exception of industries where a clear and objective piece rate could be set, such as among bricklayers, the pay system often involved a high degree of favoritism and subjectivity.

While the subject of compensation is a very large territory indeed, Gary Gardiner and O. C. Ferrell commented on the matter by distinguishing the *political* from the *competent* organization.[10] While the word "political" can have many positive connotations, such as willingness to compromise and to save face, to many of us it means negative things like manipulative and dishonest. The classic political organization in American life has been the patronage office, where all jobs are determined by a favorable connection with the duly elected officeholder. It is not *what* you know but *who* you know that matters, and if the head of the organization fails to win re-election, all the jobholders go out together.

In the *competent* organization on the other hand—and we find these in the private and public sectors—employees are rewarded for competence, creativity, and value creation. In other words, *their compensation is tied to their ability to create value for their organizations.* In their classic volume, *In Search of Excellence*, Peters and Waterman noted that America's excellent companies often make use of compensation schemes such as profit sharing and bonuses for productivity, which are designed to reward their most competent workers: In other words, the people who are creating value for them.[11]

There are several examples of highly effective compensation systems that will enhance value creation, some of which have already been referred to in these pages. *Profit sharing* in various forms has a long history in American industry, and has or is being used at such well-known companies as Hewlett-Packard, Ford, General Motors, Alcoa, Caterpillar, Monsanto, and AT & T. Most of these plans replace some portion of an employee's base salary with the potential to earn shares of the profits, so there is some downside risk for the employee. Two arguments are generally made in favor of profit sharing: (1) It encourages employees to think like owners, take a broad view of the organization's needs, and produce increased cooperation and citizenship as the result. (2) Since profit-sharing payments are not part of base pay, labor costs are automatically reduced during economic downturns, thus reducing the need to rely on layoffs to reduce costs, and thereby significantly reducing the terrible stress and organizational trauma that always accompanies such layoffs. According to authors in the human-resource field, profit-sharing plans have a mixed history: they do not always seem to be clearly related to organizational performance, and the downside risk for employees who accept lower base pay may serve as a demotivator in tough times.[12]

Employee stock ownership plans, or *ESOPs*, have already been discussed in Chapter 5, and while they surely are not a cure-all, their steady growth throughout the decade of the 1990s indicates that they are here to stay. The number of employees in such plans grew from 4 million in 1980 to 10 million in 1992 in the United States, although growth has flattened somewhat in the late 1990s.[13] The virtues of ESOPs are fairly clear: employee ownership carries with it a sense of responsibility, a concern for the long-term welfare of the organization, and better human relations throughout the firm since in an ESOP all employees are also owners. Although some of the nation's finest firms have a significant degree of employee ownership, including Microsoft, Coca-Cola, Hewlett-Packard, and Southwest Airlines, there is no guarantee of value creation simply because of this fact, as Jeff Gates points out in *The Ownership Solution*.[14] ESOPs, he notes, have a mixed record when they are used to save companies that are already in bad financial shape, but this reality must be offset by the fact that the vast majority of such firms would have undoubtedly gone under if their employees had not taken over ownership. There is simply no question that when employees buy out a troubled firm, they are mightily motivated to save it, since their own futures are also dependent on its fate.

Gainsharing plans differ somewhat from profit sharing in that they typically attempt to measure group or plant performance, rather than the performance of the entire company, and gains in productivity are shared with employees following an agreed-upon formula. Such plans have been around for decades, and the Scanlon plan, which was developed in the 1930s by Joseph N. Scanlon at Empire Steel and Tin Plant in Mansfield, Ohio, is undoubtedly the best known of the bunch. A number of studies indicate that such plans typically have a positive impact on performance, including increased productivity, reduced rework and waste, more cost-saving suggestions, and better product quality. The organizational conditions that seem to be necessary for successful gainsharing are interesting.

> Commonly mentioned factors include (1) management commitment, (2) a need to change or a strong commitment to continuous improvement, (3) management's acceptance and encouragement of employee input, (4) high levels of cooperation and interaction, (5) employment security, (6) information sharing on productivity and costs, (7) goal setting, (8) commitment of all involved parties to the process of change and improvement, and (9) agreement on a performance standard and calculation that is understandable, seen as fair, and closely related to managerial objectives.[15]

These conditions and factors seem to be highly correlated with the organizational conditions that the authors have been arguing are necessary to create value.

As more and more companies continue to make use of project teams and other types of self-directed work groups (the percentage of all employees who now spend some or all of their time working in such groups has increased steadily and significantly over the past 20 years), *group incentives and team awards* are becoming an increasingly important form of compensation. Such awards are contingent upon team or group performance, of course, when and where it is possible and practical to measure group performance. As is the case with gainsharing plans, cost savings and successful completion of product designs and products, are typical output measures that team and group awards are based on. A growing body of research shows that if teams are to be successful, team leaders and members must not only be compensated fairly, and paid for team performance, but the teams must be constituted carefully, and be given extensive training. W. Alan Randolph, a professor of management at the University of Baltimore who does extensive work as a management consultant in the area of work-team effectiveness, has addressed this issue in an article entitled "Navigating the Journey to Empowerment" published in *Organizational Dynamics*:

> When teams are created and called upon to make important management decisions, many otherwise skillful people are often at a loss as to how to function as part of a responsible, high-performing management team. (Several of my client firms) dealt with this issue by providing extensive team training. They taught team decision making, conflicts as positive phenomena, and team goal setting and self monitoring, as well as how teams could take responsibility for leading themselves. Over a yearlong set of training experiences, coupled with on-the-job activities, individuals at these companies jelled into self-managed teams.[16]

Self-directed work teams can be a powerful means of creating value, but Randolph's experience shows that they are no quick fix. A full year of training was necessary to allow them to develop their full potential.

Executive and managerial compensation plans are also vitally important in the value-creation equation. During the 1990s more and more companies began tying executive and managerial compensation to the organization's profitability and stock performance, typically de-emphasizing base salary while developing a variety of stock option packages for senior company officials that would be triggered when the firm's profitability or share price reached a certain point. The logic of these plans was to encourage executives to create shareholder value, which is in itself a short-term process, but the plans ran into problems because of a phenomenon that few business analysts predicted or expected: the great bull stock market of the late 1990s. Many executives were earning large bonuses, and cashing in millions and millions of dollars worth of stock options, even though their firms were not outperforming the bull market. By 1995 the average CEO of a Fortune 500 company was earning about 117 times as much as the average employee of that company, a multiple that had increased from 35 times in 1975. These happy souls were cashing in on a bull market that had created shareholder value, but in many cases their companies were not doing all that well relative to the market. At the time of this writing, the issue of executive compensation and its relation to value creation is a hot topic, and many companies are beginning to consider alternatives to the stock-option packages that seemed so attractive and reasonable only a few years earlier. In the final analysis, all employees must be compensated in line with their value-creating capacity for the organization and the individual to reach their value-creating potential. If organizations do not figure it out, the market will often determine the solution.

Step 4: Restructuring

Step 4 in implementing Value Driven Management involves *restructuring the organization as needed to facilitate value creation.* The good old-fashioned hierarchical, vertical, and functional approach to organizing a business and its operations made sense at a time when most work processes were fairly simple, when workers were poorly educated, and when life was fairly static and stable. In the new millennium, such relatively rigid organizational structures do not make good sense because the world has changed. Throughout American industry, and around the globe, new organizational models are emerging that depart significantly from the familiar boxes and lines that we associate with organization charts.

The new models take many forms, and contain numerous variations, but they have some common features, which Gary Gardiner described at length in *21st Century Manager.*[17] While many of these emerging models may already be familiar to many readers, it may well prove worthwhile to review some of the things they have in common:

1. There are fewer layers of authority or command. These organizations are flatter, often decentralized, and less encumbered by bureaucratic barriers within the organization.

2. The firm is organized around *work processes*, and much or all of the work is carried out by work teams or project teams. For example, Eastman Chemicals' organizational chart for its up-state New York plant (see Figure 6-2) resembles a pizza, because the entire plant is made of up empowered work teams—represented by the "pepperoni" in the chart—who have major responsibility for planning, organizing, and actually doing work. Staff support groups have equal status with work teams, and there is no functional hierarchy as such.[18]

3. The role of the manager and management becomes more that of a facilitator or coach, and less that of a "boss." Empowered employees and work teams are treated as responsible adults, who have enough intelligence and common sense to organize and direct themselves.

4. Problem-solving and analytic thinking skills are at a premium throughout the organization. Given the complexity of much of the work carried out by contemporary firms, the ability of employees—all employees—to think for themselves, and to process information in a sophisticated way, is of crucial importance. There is a tremendous shortage of such people in the American workplace, and hundreds of thousands of jobs go unfilled each year because of that fact. Yet there is still a surplus—even in a full-employment economy—of unskilled workers.

This has been a thumbnail sketch, admittedly, of the changes that are occurring in contemporary organizations, but these are organizational themes that will continue in the decades to come. Both authors are frequently asked by students, businesspersons, and colleagues why such changes have been painstakingly slow in many cases, and while there is no single answer as to why organizational change can be so difficult, there are several reasons that can be cited: (1) The age-old problem of mindsets and file folders—"We've always done it that way" or "Every worker needs to have a boss." (2) The reluctance to give up managerial authority and power. Empowerment requires not only a loosening of the reins of authority, but an attitude of genuine respect and caring for other employees in the organization. Power is addictive and compulsive for many traditional managers, and it is a

Figure 6-2 Traditional versus emerging organizational models.

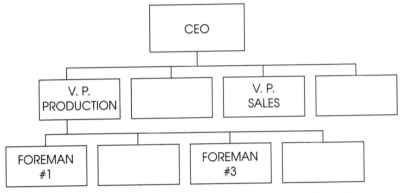

A traditional, hierarchical, functional organization chart

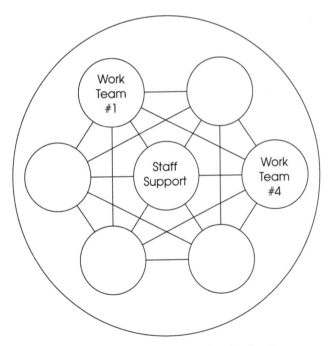

Eastman Chemicals' "pizza" chart

real gut wrench to give it up. (3) Unwillingness to give participative and open management more time to work. In a society hooked on quick fixes, many noble experiments are abandoned before they have had a fair chance to work. The result of abandoned initiatives is often an "I told you so" attitude accompanied by a return to traditional and authoritarian management methods. Both authors promise to preach no more sermons on this particular topic, but both would like to insert a gentle reminder at this point that value creation occurs much more often in open and participative organizations than in hierarchical and bureaucratic ones.

Step 5: Employee Selection

Step 5 is *the systematic and organization-wide selection of employees who will create value in the positions they fill*. The heavy emphasis that Koch Industries places on the careful selection of employees whose values will be congruent with its corporate culture is central to its success, and it is hardly surprising that other excellent companies also take great pains to hire people who will make outstanding employees and create value for themselves and the organization for which they work. Southwest Airlines, an organization mentioned often in these pages, is just such a company. Southwest is rigorous and painstaking in its selection process.

In addition to the high motivation and expectations for performance, evidence of the company culture can be seen in the recruitment and selection process. Southwest accepts applications for ground operations positions or as flight attendants all year round. Many of the applicants are Southwest customers who have seen recruitment ads like the one featuring [Herb] Kelleher dressed as Elvis. In 1994, Southwest received more than 126,000 applications for a variety of positions; the People Department interviewed more than 35,000 individuals for 4,500 positions. . . . This large labor pool allows the company to hire employees who most closely fit a cul-

ture in which they are asked to use their own judgment
and to go beyond "the job description."[19]

The front-end expense of accepting thousands of applications,
and interviewing thousands and thousands of individuals for
jobs, Southwest believes, is more than compensated for down-
stream by the value that is created by the talented men and
women who are eventually selected for these vital positions in the
company.

Randy Pohlman had the good fortune of being able to devote
a large chunk of his time to employee selection and development
at Koch Industries during his term there, and Koch spends every
bit as much time as does Southwest Airlines on this vital component of creating value. The Koch process begins with the company's vision or mission statement, as well as its statement of
business philosophy, reproduced in Chapter 5. These statements
give both current and prospective employees a "feel" for the type
of organization and people with whom they are working, or will
work with. The next step is developing a set of principles or value
dimensions that will help guide the behavior of existing employees, and aid in the selection of new ones. The technique of brainstorming using a group of value-creating employees, which is
described later in this chapter, is an effective method of identifying the characteristics of people with whom these key employees
would like to work. The characteristics that emerge from the
brainstorming session can then be turned into a list of principles
or value dimensions.

Once principles or value dimensions have been identified,
and are understood by employees, they can be used to develop
behavioral-interview questions for prospective employees. Behav-
ioral interviewing is based on the straightforward and commonsensical premise that peoples' past behavior is the best predictor
of their future behavior, and the questions that are asked in be-
havioral interviews are designed to stimulate the interviewee to
discuss his or her previous behavior in coping with a variety of
work-related problems and situations. A significant amount of
training in this technique is required if it is to be used effectively,
but it can be mastered by most people involved in the interview
process. The behavioral-interview technique provides examples

of past interviewee behavior that can be compared by the interviewer to behavior that is expected in the organization. The interviewer or interviewers can then decide if there will be a fit between the prospective employee's behavior and values and the company's expectations that goes beyond the technical requirements of the position.

The list of principles or value dimensions can also be a powerful tool in facilitating employee development. Employees should be encouraged to take responsibility for internalizing the value dimensions, and for practicing them, as well as for improving their technical qualifications—technical training has traditionally been the major or only component of employee development. As employees become more and more competent and confident in using value dimensions in conjunction with technical skills, and begin to make decisions that are truly value adding, they must also be given expanded decision rights: the right to make more and more decisions of significance to the organization. Employees will achieve their full potential only when their expanded decision rights are also accompanied by compensation that is commensurate with the value they are creating, and with their value in the marketplace.

Step 6: Emphasis on Value Creation

Step 6 is *to make value creation the topic of the day, every day.* Like the periodic great American religious revival, where the faithful are gathered together on key occasions by their leaders to have their faith rejuvenated and fortified, Value Driven Management also requires periodic rites of renewal. Organizational culture is a living, breathing entity that exists within the hearts and minds of the organization's members, but it is also a part of the firm's history, and it is supported and reinforced by corporate rituals and company legends, such as all the stories that employees at Nordstrom or American Express like to tell about the heroic service that they have performed for customers.

Herb Kelleher of Southwest Airlines clearly recognizes the importance of keeping his firm's vibrant culture alive by holding regular parties where Southwest employees revel in their company's excellence and celebrate their common sense of mission and purpose. These celebrations have become part of South-west's legend—part of the collective consciousness of all its em-ployees. Kelleher's genius has reached full flower in this area. After nearly 30 years of existence, the corporate culture at South-west Airlines is probably more dynamic than ever.

There is no single recipe that we know of for keeping a cor-porate culture alive and well, but one rule that companies might well keep in mind is *to make celebrations, however elaborate or subtle as they may be, as spontaneous as possible,* and *tie celebra-tions to real achievements and accomplishments, not only immedi-ate profitability.* The creative and value-driven organization will consistently find creative and value-creating ways of recognizing and rewarding organizational achievement, whether that achieve-ment be a highly profitable fiscal year, a successful new product launch, or winning a Baldrige quality award. Impromptu parties to celebrate excellence have become a way of life at Southwest Airlines, but parties, of course, are not the only vehicle of celebra-tion. They also use spontaneous gifts to employees, dramatically unfurling banners and flags, "field days" at the ball park or sym-phony hall, and occasional award ceremonies to help keep Value Driven Management alive and well.

Making value creation the topic of the day is a positive and visible way of reaffirming belief in a philosophy that makes sense, and will pay off for the organization in the long haul. Periodic reaffirmation, especially when this can be accomplished in novel and unusual ways, limited only by the imaginations of its spon-sors, has a long and distinguished history in keeping human faith and culture alive, and nowhere is this more true than in main-taining a powerful organizational culture.

Step 7: Lifelong Education

Step 7 is so important in implementing and using Value Driven Management in an organization that it transcends and unifies steps 1 through 6. It is *the ongoing, comprehensive, and lifelong education of all the employees of the organization in the balancing act: How to use Value Driven Management in the organizational decision-making process.* Throughout the 1990s, organizations of every type began to invest more and more money in every type of

training: technical training, often involving the use of sophisticated new computer packages; on-the-job training for new and
relocated employees; training in high-performance management
and managing for quality; training in a host of leadership and
management skills; and training in better interpersonal, team-
building, and customer-relations skills. Training took off in the
1990s because organizations began to realize that they needed
not only to maintain, but to upgrade the skills of valuable employees if they were to increase organizational productivity.

Three new phrases in the training field became popular:
high-leverage training, a *learning organization,* and *continuous
learning.*[20] High-leverage training is training that has a clear link-
age to the organization's strategic goals, results from careful design and evaluation, and has top management's support. A
learning organization is a firm which has adopted a philosophy
of continuous improvement, and where formal training is only
one phase of a process of critical thinking and evaluation. Continuous learning is just what the name implies: Employees are expected to continuously acquire new skills, but also become
familiar with the organization's business goals and objectives. Organization-wide training in Value Driven Management is all three
of these: It is high-leverage because it is strategic, it occurs in a
learning organization, and it is lifelong learning.

It also has, as a major goal, the moving of all the members of
the organization from (1) unconscious incompetence, through (2)
conscious incompetence and (3) conscious competence, until
they reach (4) unconscious competence in terms of their ability
to process information, think analytically, and make intelligent
decisions.[21] The consciousness/competence dimension is a qua-
dratic form of analysis originally developed by Harvard psychologist Jerome Bruner, and which has been widely used in the
training field. This model is highly relevant to the implementation
and application of Value Driven Management because it demonstrates so clearly how we move from awkwardness and incompetence to skillfulness and confidence.

In the first stage, when individuals are in a state of *unconscious incompetence,* they simply are unaware that they are incompetent in a particular area. For example, if you were not
aware of the highly popular in-line skating phenomenon, you

would not only be incompetent in in-line skating, but you would also be totally unaware that you are incompetent. Ignorance is bliss, as the saying goes. In the next stage of *conscious incompetence*, individuals are aware that there is such a competency, but they have not yet developed it. When one is trying to learn a new skill or sport, for example, this can be a very awkward and painful stage. During the conscious/incompetent phase of growth, one is trying to learn the fundamentals or basics, put them together to form a complete whole, and become functional in that skill or sport. During this stage, since there is a very steep learning curve, many mistakes will be made, and a person will often feel confused and ineffective. This is normal behavior during this stage, since growth is not always blissful—it is often stressful and painful. The person may skate safely for a few steps, but falls are still frequent.

In the *conscious/competent* stage, the individual has achieved a certain level of competence, but a great deal of concentration is still required, and a person must still pay careful attention to all the fundamental skills that are required. During this stage one must be very conscious of every step in the process in order to reach their newly acquired level of competence. The in-line skater now skates carefully and slowly, but falls are becoming infrequent. At this stage, individuals are less skilled and slower than they will be when they finally reach the level of competence to which they aspire.

Finally, when an individual has reached the highest level— *unconscious competence*—the competency they have now attained becomes intuitive and natural, and does not require conscious effort or analysis. The in-line skater now skates swiftly and gracefully, and swoops and swerves with creative joy and abandon. As we reflect upon these four stages of growth, and begin thinking of new sport skills or management techniques we have learned, the validity and power of Bruner's model becomes even more apparent. The model applies neatly and powerfully to the implementation of Value Driven Management. At first, just reading about it may be awkward. It may seem to us that it would require too much time and effort to be effective. This is a normal reaction, however, to change and growth, and to achieving higher levels of competence.

In teaching individuals and teams in the organization to use Value Driven Management in their thinking and decision making, we can expect that many persons and teams will be at the level of unconscious incompetence, and we must further expect that it may be a long and sometimes painful struggle until the entire organization reaches the level of unconscious competence. To help our readers begin to visualize how to use Value Driven Management to create value for themselves and for their organization, and become ever more confident and skillful, we have represented the model graphically in Figure 6-3, with each value driver balanced on a "merry-go-round." As the merry-go-round rotates at varying rates of speed, each value driver may go up or down in importance as the organization contemplates the actions it will take in the short- and long-term.

Since all the value drivers are connected to the heart of the

Figure 6-3   The Value Driven Management merry-go-round.

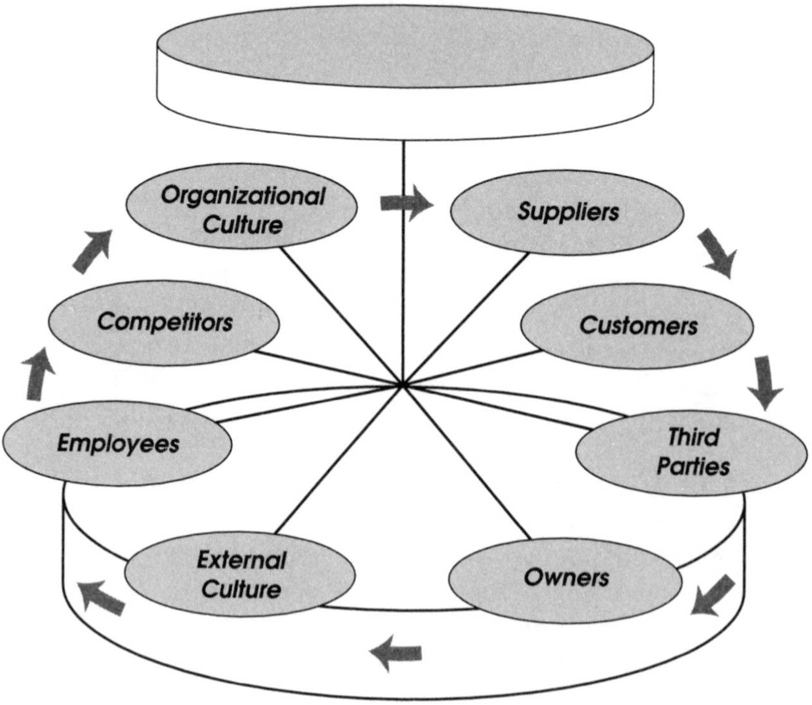

merry-go-round, and connected to each other, they must be carefully balanced and juggled so that the merry-go-round will continue to rotate smoothly. If any of the value drivers happen to get seriously out of balance, the entire machine may grind to a halt, or even destroy itself.

Developing a Training Program

The merry-go-round analogy may be interesting and compelling, but it probably begs the question of exactly what we need to do in developing a high-leverage training program for the organization. There are several steps in this process:

Identify the Key Issues

The first step is to identify the key issues involved in the decision or decisions at hand. If you are the Nordstrom department store chain, for example, and you are debating whether or not to go national or stay in your present niche as a regional chain, a key issue may be whether or not the proposed expansion is achievable given your present level of resources and your core competencies. Are there alternative strategies for expanding, if that is in fact a desirable goal? In this first stage of a major decisional process, value drivers come into play: Clearly Nordstrom felt that its long history of outstanding customer service would be a major asset in its ambitious expansion plans, but it may have overlooked the fact that its internal culture—which it also regarded as an asset—might be a serious problem, short- and long-term, in going national. Identifying key issues can often be dealt with effectively using the brainstorming technique to get key issues on the table, or the nominal group technique to rank order and prioritize issues.

In what Gary Gardiner has termed "proactive team brainstorming" the best features of both conventional brainstorming and the nominal group technique are combined in the following series of steps:

1. The team leader states a problem to be brainstormed and asks members of the group to think of possible solutions.

2. Group members share ideas verbally (one at a time after being recognized by the team leader, without interruption, and *without discussion*). The team leader records the ideas on a chart or board for ten to fifteen minutes.

3. The group discusses the list of ideas for about 15 minutes.

4. Each group member *rank orders* the best five ideas the group has produced.

5. The team leader *tabulates* rank-ordering data.

6. In the final phase, the team leader asks the group to finalize their choice for the *best* solution, and the best available *back-up* solution.[22]

The more open and widespread this type of process is in the organization, the better, of course. The brainstorming approach to decision making is exactly the sort of technique that frees the organization's members to begin discussing ideas—all ideas—openly, and in a way that will lead to the development of multidimensional thinking and alternative solutions.

Determine the Most Important Value Drivers

The second step is to determine which value drivers are most important for maximizing value over time in this decisional context. If you are Johnson & Johnson, for example, and you are stunned to discover that a maniac is poisoning one of your most popular products, do customer values become critically important in your decisional process, particularly as you begin to think what the effects of your decision will be over the long haul? In any given decision-making situation, one or several value drivers may outweigh others.

Evaluate Each Value Driver

The third step is to evaluate each value driver from three points of view or dimensions. Each value driver should be evaluated and analyzed to:

1. Identify specific aspects of the situation and how they relate to the value driver. If you are Exxon, what legal and environ-

mental concerns do you now face since your oil tanker just ran aground?

2. Enumerate the potential impact of each specific aspect of the problem—positive and negative—on value over time, both short- and long-term. If you are Johnson & Johnson, is your long-term relationship with your customers the most important aspect of your decision whether to withdraw your product from retail shelves?

3. Consider actions you can take to turn negative effects of an aspect into positive ones. If your customers are frightened by the possibility of buying poisoned capsules, a reassuring public statement by your CEO that you will pull the product immediately might become a major plus for you because it demonstrates a genuine concern for your customers' welfare and safety.

Consider Unintended Consequences

The fourth step is to consider any and all of the unintended consequences that might result from your proposed decision or actions. You never thought of the possibility, you say, that your new high-tech super-hard graphite football helmet, which you designed to protect the wearer's head, could also be a lethal battering ram, and lead to large and expensive lawsuits—and reams and reams of bad publicity—after several players are killed when struck by it? The point has already been made in this volume that the most effective way of dealing with the possibility of unintended consequences is to sit down, think about them, and then set them down—in writing, if possible. This process seems so necessary and commonsensical that it is amazing how often organizations simply fail to carry it out, and then later are stunned by the havoc their product or decision creates.

Carry Out the Balancing Act

The final step is to carry out the balancing act. In every decision and contemplation of an action or actions, have you overlooked anything? Have you considered all the value drivers that might be important in your decision? Have you thought things through, short- and long-term? Are there unintended consequences that might result from your decision? Have you given detailed thoughts of your decisional process? Have you taken time to mull the decision over until it feels intuitively right? Have you avoided a compulsive and hasty decision that was made simply to reduce stress? Has this all been done within the context of maximizing value over time for your organization?

A Strategic Note on Organizational Training in Value Driven Management

It is simply a reality that if training in Value Driven Management is to create real value for the organization using it, every organization must develop its own cases, exercises, decision-making paradigms, and scenarios for analysis. At Nova Southeastern University such a series of learning experiences has been under development for several years now, for use in the university's MBA program, which is integrated and unified by the value-driven philosophy. An initial evaluation of the MBA curriculum indicates that graduating students find it valuable, enlightening, and a powerful tool for use in their personal and organizational lives. Several more studies are currently underway, with the goal of improving and refining the current curriculum.

A strategic note on implementation is to *start at the top and start at the bottom.* Top management support is vital to success, as we have stated many times, but the support of employees is also vital for building energy and commitment, and making Value Driven Management come alive. Middle management is truly in the middle when it comes to implementing organizational change, since middle managers often bear the brunt of changes in managerial process and philosophy, and for this reason they are often the last people in the organization to "get on board" when change occurs. The experience of the authors in implementing change is that the top-and-bottom model is superior to any other if real change is to occur, and be sustainable.

Round and Round on the Merry-Go-Round

The Value Driven Management merry-go-round is truly a vehicle that never stops, except once in a while for vital maintenance. So it is with organizations that compete in free markets, that have determined competitors who also never rest, and that must continuously strive for excellence. The merry-go-round may grind to a halt in an amazing hurry, however, if it gets seriously out of balance: if the organization loses sight of what its customers want, for example, as Levi Strauss did in the late 1990s. The discipline of the marketplace can humble even the mightiest company in an astoundingly brief period of time, as the IBM colossus discovered to its dismay in the early 1990s. Value Driven Management is a philosophy that will allow a company to stay balanced, and alert, and alive. Value Driven Management will not *guarantee* an organization's success, of course, since there are no such guarantees available in the marketplace; but its systematic, conscientious, and long-term use will create and maximize value over time for every organization using it, we believe. Its systematic and effective use can also maximize value in our personal lives, interestingly, and that is the topic that we shall cover in the final chapter of this book.

Case 6-1

Mark Twain Business Consultant*
by James Champy

How do YOU REACT when your car goes into a skid? If experience takes over, you pump the brakes. With today's antilock brakes, that's the wrong move. You're supposed to mash the pedal and let the computer-driven mechanism flutter the brakes.

Experience can be a trap in a crisis. When successful companies start to spin out of control, the self-assured executives who run them instinctively reach for the tried-and-true like the fellow who pumps his antilock brakes. The classic example is IBM in the early 1990s. Chief Executive John Akers sold mainframes as a young man, and his experience was so

---

*Reprinted by Permission of Forbes Magazine ©1999 Forbes 1997.[23]

much involved with big iron that he let the PC revolution pass him by. It took Lou Gerstner, a man with no computer industry experience, to inject real change into this giant company. Unlike Akers, Gerstner wasn't conditioned to pump the brakes.

Ceaseless change continues to bedevil the technology industry with counterintuitive lessons. Microsoft's attempt to build a proprietary on-line service—Microsoft Network initially bombed. Not for lack of great features, but because the Internet's ''open systems'' bias was foreign to Microsoft's reaction pattern of proprietary control.

How do you avoid these pitfalls of experience? First, don't assume that because your instincts served you well in the past they will do so today. Remember the lessons of evolution: Creatures beautifully conditioned to flourish in one environment often perish when their environment changes.

If you suspect your environment is changing, and your sensing capabilities aren't telling you what to do, get help fast. If you're a retail banker and you find out that an Internet-based ''virtual bank'' can process transactions at one-tenth the cost of your real-estate-based empire, hire some kids from a software products company. Be humble. Listen to what they say even if it conflicts with everything experience has taught you. These kids may have a clearer vision of the future than you have.

Think of ways to put yourself out of business with new products before your competitor beats you to the punch. Each generation of Intel's microprocessors is an exercise in planned obsolescence that resets the performance bar. Product developers at IBM used to call this ''eating your babies,'' and it was against the culture. Too bad for IBM. What worked well for several decades suddenly stopped working.

Read stuff that's totally unrelated to your industry. An energy executive got the idea for electricity auctions from an article in a computer publication. Hallmark designers, accustomed to sugar-sweet stuff, crated the irreverent ''Shoe Box'' line of cards using topics culled from the *National Inquirer*—not Hallmark's usual source of inspiration. It was a big success.

Finally—and this may sound heretical in a time when everyone pays lip service to ''listening to the customer''—I've found you simply cannot trust what customers say they want. Instead, study their habits and everyday experiences, their frustrations and failures. When Lexus designed its sales and service systems, Toyota didn't poll car buyers. It employed anthropologists to study car salesrooms. They watched customers cringe whenever the salesman approached. So Lexus designed sales centers where customers could gawk, try out the seats and kick the tires on their own. The salespeople wait until they are summoned. In its first year, Lexus drove past some very fast company—Mercedes, Porsche and BMW—to become number one in customer satisfaction.

The very wise Mark Twain never saw a computer, but he has smart advice for executives in the computer age. More than a century ago he understood the dangers of blindly trusting past experience for dealing with the future. ''We should be careful to get out of an experience only the wisdom that is in it,'' Twain wrote, ''and stop there, lest we be like the cat that sits down on a hot stove lid. She will not sit down on a hot stove lid again—but also she will never sit down on a cold one anymore.''

Questions for Discussion and Reflection

1. Throughout this volume, the authors have referred to file folders and mindsets. When noted author James Champy (coauthor of *Reengineering the Corporation*) talks about the pitfalls of experience, do you suspect he might be talking about very much the same thing?

2. Champy says, "If you suspect your environment is changing, and your sensory capabilities aren't telling you what to do, get help fast." Does this sound like a sensible technique for thinking-out-of-the-box and creating value for your organization?

3. Why does Champy tell us to "read stuff that's totally unrelated" to the industry we are working in? Champy quotes Mark Twain on the value of trusting past experience as a guide for making decisions in the future. In view of this, how would you evaluate the old adage, "Experience is the best teacher?"

4. Champy also mentions the fact that everyone pays lip service to "listening to the customer." To create real customer value, he suggests that we must go far beyond listening. How do you feel about his suggestions for identifying and anticipating customer wants and needs?

Endnotes

1. See Harold M. Schroder, Michael Driver, and Siegfried Streufert, *Human Information Processing* (New York: McGraw-Hill, 1967).
2. Seanna Browder, "Great Service Wasn't Enough," *Business Week*, 19 April 1999, 126–127.
3. Ibid., 126.
4. Ibid., 127.
5. Ibid.
6. Roberto C. Goizueta, "Why Shareowner Value?" *The CEO Series*, no. 13 (St. Louis, MO: Center for the Study of American Business, 1997), 5.

7. Rensis Likert, *New Patterns of Management* (New York: McGraw-Hill, 1961).

8. Rensis Likert, *The Human Organization* (New York: McGraw-Hill, 1967).

9. Ibid.

10. O. C. Ferrell and Gareth S. Gardiner, *In Pursuit of Ethics* (Springfield, IL: Smith Collins, 1991), 87–89.

11. Thomas J. Peters and Robert H. Waterman, Jr., *In Search of Excellence* (New York: Harper & Row, 1982).

12. Raymond Noe, John Hollenbeck, Barry Gerhart, and Patrick Wright, *Human Resource Management*, 2nd ed. (Boston: Irwin/McGraw-Hill, 1996), 497–499.

13. Ibid., 499–501.

14. Jeffrey R. Gates, *The Ownership Solution* (Reading, MA: Addison-Wesley, 1998).

15. Noe et al., *Human Resource Management*, 503.

16. W. Alan Randolph, "Navigating the Journey to Empowerment," *Organizational Dynamics*, spring 1995, 19–32.

17. Gareth S. Gardiner, *21st Century Manager* (Princeton, NJ: Peterson's/Pacesetter Books, 1996).

18. Ibid.

19. Noe et al., *Human Resource Management*, 159.

20. Ibid., 341.

21. Jerome S. Bruner, *Beyond the Information Given: Studies in the Psychology of Knowing* (New York: Norton, 1973).

22. Gardiner, *21st Century Manager*, 136.

23. James Champy, "Mark Twain, Business Consultant," *Forbes*, 11 August 1997, 103–104.

Chapter 7

What's in It for Me? Value Driven Management and Personal Happiness

Maximizing personal value over time, we believe, is first and foremost the responsibility of each individual. In the changing American and global workplace, where traditional job roles have changed irreversibly, a host of new opportunities have arisen for men and women to maximize value for themselves in the new work environments that are springing up everywhere. The traditional notion of the relationship between employer and employee, where the employer was a loving parent responsible for looking after a loyal but dependent child for a lifetime, has gone by the boards, and a new workplace ethic is emerging where consenting adults engage in a consensual relationship to create value, and where each—employer and employee—are responsible for their portion of the contract. Each man or woman in the workplace is not only responsible for the conditions of his or her employment, but is also responsible for personal career development—whether or not there is enough value congruency with the employer and conditions of employment to continue a relationship with that employer. It is in the very best of ways, a brave new world.

Work is one of the major psychological, emotional, mental, physical, metaphorical, and continuing themes in the lives of working people all over the globe. What we are trying to say is that work is very important to almost all of us! In the course of the average lifetime, the only activity that consumes more time than a person's job or career is sleep. The average workweek in the United States, for people at every level of employment, regularly exceeds 40 hours. Jobs are a major source of self-esteem—or lack of self-esteem—and personal identity. When we meet a new person, and ask a routine social question like, "And what do you do?" the answer is almost always something like, "Oh, I'm an accountant at Caterpillar," or "I've worked for Florida Power and Light over 20 years." People tend to identify themselves, first and foremost, with their occupations.

Most working men and women want to be proud of their jobs, themselves, and their employers—and millions are. Professional engineers speak with pride about their ability to build sound structures or design good and durable highways. Career women, whose numbers now nearly equal the number of men in the workplace in the United States, take great satisfaction in being able to juggle and balance the demands of a full-time profession with the challenges of parenthood (as, of course, do working fathers). This balancing act carried out every year by millions of working women and men may surpass in complexity any balancing act previously described in these pages, and represents a major source of value creation in American society, and around the globe. Millions and millions of young Americans, most still in their teens, work part- or full-time while they study toward graduation from high school or college. The work ethic is alive and well in contemporary America, despite the cries of an occasional doomsayer.

Many Americans also comment in survey after survey that they enjoy their work, enjoy their managers and coworkers, and that their job or profession is a positive force in their lives. It not only generates income, but also generally provides them with a high level of self-esteem and psychological satisfaction. The flip side of this, of course, is the millions of Americans who detest, and also fear that they will lose, their jobs. This last number varies anywhere from 30 to 50 percent, depending on how and when a survey is taken. It is sad when a hard-working secretary, whose supervisor heavily depends upon her to keep the office functioning, describes herself as "just a secretary." Unfortunately, our jobs, professions, and careers, can also be powerful negative forces in our lives. One of the important purposes of this final chapter of Value Driven Management is to develop a series of self-help activities to help move what we do for a living to a more value-creating and positive force in our passage through this existence—a force for growth, high self-esteem, and even self-actualization.

The Changing Nature of the Workplace and Workforce

In the mid-1990s, Compaq Computer sent its sales force home. The firm's sales offices were closed and each salesperson was given a computer and told that they would immediately begin working out of their homes. Each computer was networked with access to databases containing virtually up-to-the-minute information on company clients upon whom salespeople might make a call. The sales force was also downsized significantly to two thirds of its former size, but after two years of home-based calls, the firm's revenues doubled at a time when the price per unit of personal computers was falling sharply. Arno Penzias, writing in *Fortune* magazine, noted that productivity over this period—as measured in computers sold per salesperson—increased by 600 percent.[1] The sales force reported that it was working longer and harder than ever before, but it also reported that freedom from management controls and demands, internal bureaucracy, and time wasted in meetings, was resulting in greater job satisfaction than ever before.

When Compaq bought Digital Equipment Corporation for $8.4 billion in January 1998, it was supposedly a defining moment in the computer industry. The deal failed to produce the promised dividends, however, and one reason was the difficulty of merging very different corporate cultures. The failure of many mergers and acquisitions to create promised value is both interesting and complex, but the poor performance and subsequent dismemberment of many merged companies challenges one of our most cherished myths: that growth is *always* good, and will *always* create value. Growth is, of course, a mighty engine for propelling companies forward, and creating value. It can also create chaos when it occurs without much strategic planning, when it is the result of executive *hubris*, resulting in far too much being paid for an acquired company, and when the merged firms are in industries that do not have much in common.

When Compaq ran slightly off course and fired CEO Eckhard Pfeiffer in April 1999, the problem, however, was not lack of motivation of the sales force. Indeed, Compaq's reassignment of its sales force to their respective homes was a harbinger of things to come—more and more American men and women working out of their homes, with the blessing of their employers and almost always making use of advanced computer technology. As the turn of the century approached, some 15 million Americans had been empowered to *telecommute*: Without exception they did so in industries where high-tech support made telecommuting feasible. While most found the experience positive and uplifting, many also suffered from feelings of loneliness, and missed the social contact that most workers take for granted as the result of working out of an office.

As telecommuting continued to grow in popularity late in the century, the trend toward flattening of organizations also continued to grow, as did the percentage of employees assigned to self-directed work teams. These trends began to change the role of the manager from boss to coach, as we have already noted, but they also changed the whole notion of what constitutes a career, and what career development is. Arno Penzias was one of the first commentators to pick up on this in the mid-1990s. In "New Paths to Success," he stated that one of the clear implications of the trend away from hierarchical organizations would be the fact that managers and employees would become more *generalists* than *specialists*, with managers spending more and more time working across a horizontal ladder, working with teams and individuals from many different units within the organization.[2]

Individuals would also, for the large part, forsake the traditional career that employees were accustomed to in American industry—a lifetime career with one firm, with periodic promotions up a vertical ladder. In the flat organization, organized around projects and teams, any promotions available would be the direct result of an individual's increased *competence*: a person's increased versatility, flexibility, and usefulness, resulting from the development of multitask value-creating competencies. More and varied jobs on a horizontal ladder would be a major force in the development of such a skill set and competency profile, but so would lifelong education, not only in vital and necessary technical skills, but in the so-called *soft skills* that nearly all members of the workforce would need in such an environment: communication, conflict management, effective team-building and team-management skills, high-performance goal setting, and a host of related topics.

Two other changes in the composition of the workforce itself are worth commenting on, although they have been well documented elsewhere. One is the emergence of a much more diverse workforce than has historically been the case, both in this country and around the globe. In the United States, more and more women and members of minority groups have entered, and are entering, the workforce. By the end of the first decade of the new millennium, white males—once far and away the largest portion of the workforce, and once almost *all* of management—will have become a minority of the American workforce, although still a majority of middle- to top-level management. The so-called *glass ceiling* for women and members of minority groups with managerial aspirations is already beginning to shatter, and will soon be lying in great heaps of shards as it crumbles completely. The glass ceiling may well have resulted in part from white male prejudice or resistance to inroads from other groups, but to a greater extent it may just have been a function of time—the time women and minority-group members needed to climb the remaining rungs of the corporate ladder.[3]

The traditional concept of a full-time worker in a functional job is also beginning to go the way of the dinosaur, as companies rely more and more on cross-functional team members, part-time employees, and temporary workers. This last group, the temps, are apparently here to stay as a permanent part of the workforce.

> The number of full-time functional jobs will continue to decline, as more and more workers and managers enter the team environment, and this will result in companies' reliance on large numbers of temporary workers.

Temps will be used to perform functionally based jobs
on a temporary basis as well as to carry out whole projects. A large percentage of temps will be women—
currently 72 percent of temps are women (one third
have college degrees)—enjoying the flexibility that temporary work gives them. They will also be workers with
an *attitude* ("I'm bright, motivated, and self-disciplined.
Train me, treat me right, and leave me alone so I can
get my work done. Thank you very much.") since most
know full well that hundreds of companies are eager to
have their services.[4]

In many cases temporary workers apparently highly value independence, knowing that they can work pretty much where and
when they please; but they also enjoy *social contact* with the
friends they make in the workplace, and the temporary work arrangement frees them up to spend quality time with their *families*. As work arrangements everywhere become more flexible,
and as the workforce becomes more diverse, new opportunities
are arising almost constantly for bright men and women to maximize value for themselves in the workplace.

One of the realities of the great American economic boom of
the mid- to late-1990s, however, is that the benefits of the boom
have largely been limited to those men and women who have
upgraded their skills through continuous education and training.
In a column in *Business Week*, provocatively entitled "Why the
Wage Gap Just Keeps Getting Bigger and Bigger," Laura D'Andrea
Tyson—former chief economic advisor to President Clinton, and
now Dean of the Haas School of Business at the University of
California at Berkeley—commented that the share of the nation's
income going to the bottom 60 percent of families has continued
to fall since 1989, while the share going to the top 5 percent of
American families has reached a postwar high. She notes further,
that over the past two decades, there has been growing inequality
in the distribution of wages and salaries between and within occupations, skill levels, age groups, and educational categories.

In answering the question of why this has happened, she
focuses on education and skills:

By far the most important determinant of the growing inequality in labor incomes has been the increasing demand for workers with a high level of skills, particularly those with a college or graduate degree. Such workers, who accounted for only 26 percent of the workforce in 1997, have experienced the largest increases in compensation. In contrast, workers with a high school education or less, who accounted for about 44 percent of the 1997 workforce, have continued to see the real value of their earnings erode over time.[5]

Tyson also remarks that in the age of the information revolution, there is growing inequality *within* educational categories, and she argues that to use sophisticated technologies well ". . . requires high levels of initiative, analytical capability, and communication skills—characteristics that are unevenly distributed among individuals with the same formal education."[6] The lesson is clear: The marketplace values men and women who can think multidimensionally, who are bright and flexible, and who are willing to invest time and energy in continuously upgrading their education skills. We believe that this is an economic and cultural imperative that will not only continue, but will become even more urgent in the decades to come.

The Death of Lifetime Employment and the Birth of a New Workplace Relationship

Like it or not, the huge wave of downsizing that swept through Fortune 500 companies beginning in the mid-1980s and continuing throughout the 1990s led to two interrelated changes in workplace attitudes that also seem to be permanent. The first, not surprisingly, was the death of loyalty as American workers and companies understand that term. The second was the end of the expectation that employment with a major firm would be a lifelong proposition, given a reasonable level of competence and productivity. Loyalty was traditionally a reciprocal arrangement: companies like IBM prided themselves on their lifetime employment policy for competent people, and the competent (and grateful) people were intensely faithful to their kindly employer, right down to taking great pride in wearing the company uniform—in IBM's case, the legendary button-down white shirt.

This arrangement was functional at a time when the pace of change was still relatively slow, and giant companies like IBM dominated a stable market. When the world changed, however, and the personal computer/software revolution changed the computer world forever, traditional employer-employee relationships were no longer viable. IBM downsized, of course, because it had to. The change was painful, however, just as it was at other companies that had offered long-term commitments to employees. Robert and Judith Waterman, and Betsy Collard commented in *Harvard Business Review* on its demise: "People mourn its passing—the long-time covenant between employee and employer. We fondly remember the days when IBM could offer lifetime employment."[7] Their article, entitled, "Toward a Career-Resilient Workforce," was among the first to suggest the development of a new covenant or agreement between employers and employees, in which both share responsibilities for enhancing an employee's marketability, whether that be inside or outside the firm. This is the notion of a *career-resilient workforce*, where employers offer opportunities to workers to continuously upgrade and broaden their skills, even if this involves a greater risk that they will leave the company. For their part, employees must adopt the mindset that learning is continuous, and that their future may eventually lie elsewhere with another company.

This is a concept that is rooted in a relationship between consenting adults, where there is a significant degree of *trust*, and where there is often a contract—written or unwritten—involving a fair exchange of services. Gary Gardiner remarked upon the emergence of this phenomenon in *21st Century Manager*:

> The employee gives his or her employer an honest effort and in return receives frequent training and a chance to broaden horizons by moving easily from a functional department to a project team, for example. The employer is no longer a parent with a child as a lifetime dependent who may become even more childish (and

less marketable) over time. Parent-child bonding and loyalty is replaced by trust between adults who are enlightened enough to understand that they have a mutually beneficial interest, even if this is not always long-term.[8]

This sort of arrangement is not only perfectly aboveboard and ethical, it creates unique opportunities in companies and industries where it is used for employers and employees to create and maximize value—particularly in the long run. It also satisfies the requirements of a win-win conflict-management model: Employers win, and create value for themselves, because they develop a more highly trained and flexible workforce; but employees also win because they are more marketable, and can go on to do better elsewhere if need be.

An Exciting (and Sometimes Stressful) World of Personal Responsibility and Personal Values

Some years ago, in an article in *Inc.* magazine entitled "A Nation of Owners," William Bridges took note of the changes occurring in the workplace, and in particular focused on a process he called *dejobbing*.[9] Not surprisingly, dejobbing had its start in the computer industry, where companies like Intel, Microsoft, Sun Microsystems, and Apple have largely abandoned formal jobs and job descriptions in favor of loosely described and highly flexible "pieces of work" that fit into a larger pattern of organizational work needs. Many current workers have found this development stimulating and exciting, but it has also been extremely stressful for others, says Bridges, because they have had a traditional mindset about what a job is. Clearly, one of the mindsets that accompanies a normal job is a need for structure and direction, and a willingness to accept external control from a supervisor or manager. Being responsible for "a piece of work," on the other hand, requires that the employee have a strong sense of self-direction, and a willingness to take personal responsibility for getting that particular piece of work done.

One of the clear psychological imperatives of the new workplace is precisely the need for employees to take personal responsibility for their occupations, for identifying what they personally value, and for seeking a niche in the workplace where they are largely congruent with what the organization values. This is a major departure from traditional mindsets and file folders, and Bridges remarks on this fact in his "Nation of Owners" article, when he contends that workers everywhere need to begin thinking of themselves as contingent employees, in business for themselves, and indeed as the owners of You & Co., a microbusiness and a company of one.[10] You & Co., in every case, is an entrepreneurial venture—completely owned and operated by one person—which has a variety of talents and skills to offer employers, and which is completely responsible for developing and marketing those talents and skills.

In this view, job satisfaction and personal happiness are completely the responsibility of the individual. Maximizing personal value over time and happiness is no longer someone else's responsibility—specifically not the employer's—and each and every person has a choice in the matter. One of the assumptions in this whole process is that the workplace, and a person's career, is a major driver of personal satisfaction and fulfillment, a proposition with which we started this chapter. There are at least two logical corollaries of this assumption, and the first is that each person is responsible for choosing and developing their career. The second is that career choice and development will be more satisfactory if it is made on the basis of identifying and balancing what is personally valued. This last process may sound easy or Utopian, but in practice it is not. Indeed, the process of using a value-driven approach to maximizing happiness in a career is often difficult and stressful (and we never claimed it was not!), but the payoff is likely to be a significantly higher degree of personal happiness for the person with the patience and foresight to use it.

The psychological underpinning of personal maximization of value over time is, of course, taking responsibility for the identification and satisfaction of personal values. The well-known psychologist Nathaniel Branden, whose work we have quoted previously in these pages, has a highly pertinent comment on the whole matter in his popular volume, *The Psychology of Self-*

Esteem. After noting that motivation is a major issue or problem in psychological science, he remarks that, "The key to motivation, as we have seen, is in the realm of values. Within the context of his inherent needs and capacities as a specific kind of living organism, it is a man's premises—specifically his value premises—that determine his actions and emotions."[11]

The psychology of self-esteem begins with accepting responsibility for our personal lives. This is a psychology that is the very opposite of *fatalism*, where we believe that our lives are predetermined or controlled by external forces that we cannot alter. It is an *existential* philosophy in the best sense, because it argues that all the choices we make in our lives are our own, that they cannot be blamed on someone or something else, and further, that we have no choice but to choose. If we choose to stay with an unsatisfactory and unethical employer whose values are totally in conflict with our own, that is our choice and our responsibility. The person high in self-esteem may choose to stay in such a situation for a short period of time, while they upgrade skills and competencies to help make a proactive and fulfilling long-term career choice. But that person will stay with the present employer only in order to maximize value in the long run. Trade-offs and compromises are often a reality even in the best-managed and best-lived of human lives.

Nathaniel Branden believes that taking responsibility for our lives is the very cornerstone of self-esteem and personal growth, and this notion is a continuing theme in his best-selling book, *Taking Responsibility.*[12] American society has often been accused of being a "Teflon" society where no one is willing to take responsibility for anything, and the actions of some of our governmental and business leaders over the past three decades seem to prove the point. For every point there is a counterpoint, however, and for every action a reaction. The history of irresponsibility in American life has led to a movement, spearheaded by original thinkers like Branden, urging us to live more responsible lives. From the perspective of Value Driven Management, accepting responsibility—as we have said numerous times throughout these pages—is a powerful way of maximizing value over time, particularly in our personal lives.

In the process of taking charge of our personal lives and

determining what we value, an important step in doing so is to evaluate our personal values in relation to the organization for which we work. How congruent are our personal values with those of our organization, and how satisfied are we, overall, with our organizational lives? These are basic and powerful questions for anyone wishing to maximize personal happiness, and yet they are questions that are not always answered in a systematic way. The exercise contained in Figure 7-1 (Organizational Value Congruency and Satisfaction Scale, or OVCSS) is precisely an attempt to determine for ourselves what degree of personal satisfaction we are experiencing at work, and whether we need to begin thinking about making changes in our lives.

The exercise is to some extent self-explanatory, but a few comments might clarify it. For each of the eighteen value dimensions listed in Figure 7-1, first use a 5-point scale to determine how important each dimension or value is to you personally: "5" indicates that a dimension is highly important to you, "1" means that it is unimportant, with the other numbers in between. This number should be written down in the box that appears to the immediate right of the item, under the heading "Importance to Me." When completing this exercise, you should do it first for the job that you presently hold in order to determine how congruent you are with your job, and then do it a second time for your employing organization to see how congruent your organization is with your values. After you write down an appropriate number for one of the items under the "Importance" heading, use the same 5-point scale to determine how congruent you and your job—or your organization—are on that value or dimension. If "autonomy" is very important to you, for example, but the supervisor you have is an over-controlling Theory "X" manager who grants you virtually no autonomy, you would write a "1" under "Organizational Congruency." When you do autonomy on your second trip through the OVCSS, and you feel that your organization generally grants employees much more autonomy than your present supervisor does, you might write a "4" or even a "5" under "Organizational Congruency."

Your Satisfaction Points for this value would be 5 for your current job, since an important personal value is not well satisfied in your present position. Your Satisfaction Points for your

Figure 7-1   The organizational value congruency and satisfaction scale (OVCSS).

Value Dimension (see Appendix B for detailed descriptions)	Importance to Me (5 = high; 1 = low)		Organizational Congruency (5 = high; 1 = low)		Satisfaction Points
1. AUTONOMY		×		=	
2. CREATIVITY		×		=	
3. COMPLEXITY		×		=	
4. INTENSITY		×		=	
5. STATUS		×		=	
6. PRECISION		×		=	
7. COMPETITION		×		=	
8. PHYSICAL WORK		×		=	
9. OUTDOOR WORK		×		=	
10. SECURITY		×		=	
11. ROUTINE		×		=	
12. PEOPLE ORIENTED		×		=	
13. TEAM ORIENTED		×		=	
14. TRAVEL		×		=	
15. LEADERSHIP/ AUTHORITY		×		=	
16. MANAGING		×		=	
17. RESPONSIBILITY		×		=	
18. INDUSTRY IMAGE		×		=	

TOTAL SATISFACTION POINTS   =

organization on your second trip through the OVCSS would be much higher: either 20 or 25. The higher your total number of Satisfaction Points, the more congruent is your present job—and organization—with your personal values. The theoretical maximum of these points would be 450 if all 18 value dimensions are highly important to you, and you and your job/organization are highly congruent on all of them. For a full description of each one of these dimensions, see Appendix B at the end of the book.

In practice, of course, what appears to be objective is highly personal and subjective, and there is nothing whatever wrong with that. In general, however, the higher your score for both your present job and your organization, the greater the chance that you are maximizing personal value for yourself in your work environment. If your score for your present job is much lower than your score for your organization, you might consider looking for another job with your present employer. If both scores are low, however, you are probably in the wrong job in the wrong organization, and should develop a strategy for making a career change.

Another way of interpreting your scores on the OVCSS is to pick out those value dimensions that are highly important to you, and then work out an average of the organizational congruency scores for those dimensions for both your present job and your organization. If one or two value dimensions (like "autonomy") are critically important to you, and if your job/organization is congruent on those dimensions, the odds are good that you are maximizing personal value in your present work situation.

Multidimensional Thinking and Maximization of Personal Value

Throughout this book we have stressed that we cannot go back to a world of simplicity and absolutes, and survive. There is no going back. There is only going forward, and it is the individuals and organizations who can use multidimensional and analytic thinking in their decisional and organizational processes who will survive and prosper. In every threat there is an opportunity, and in every opportunity a threat. The opportunity to grow and thrive presents itself in a new millennium to those of us who are wise enough to continue to grow, expand our competencies, do our best to anticipate and cope with change, and remain cool-headed in the midst of the worst storms. For those of us who can, and who are willing to work hard to do so, it promises to be the most dynamic and exciting period in human history. For those who cannot, or who are unwilling, it may be a very sobering time indeed. We believe that our readers, almost without exception, are those brave people and organizations who will choose the forward path; and maximize value in their lifetimes for themselves, for everyone they work with, and for their families and friends.

Case 7-1

Joe Sizemore and Corning, Inc.: A Factory Workaholic

Joe Sizemore is a good-humored, 36-year old factory worker in Corning, Inc.'s small plant in the Blue Ridge Mountain community of Blacksburg, Virginia. The plant produces ceramic cores for catalytic converters, and shifts of workers operate around the clock. The plant is unionized, but management prefers to pay overtime—and a lot of it—to about 10 percent of its 250 workers who are willing and even eager to take on a lot of additional hours. Writing in *The Wall Street Journal*, Timothy Aeppel explains management's thinking.

> Mark R. Cates, the plant manager, says the factory prefers paying overtime to hiring more workers for several reasons. For one, training workers is a lengthy and costly process and existing workers are constantly being taught new skills, so it makes sense to cover the normal ebb and flow of orders with existing workers. Using overtime also fits the plant's philosophy, which is to stay as flexible as possible and offer workers a high degree of job security. Overtime is one thing that can get cut before management has to resort to layoffs.[13]

Joe Sizemore is one of the most willing of the workers who volunteer for overtime, and he routinely works 60 or more hours a week. Overtime begins after 40 hours. He volunteers for the overtime because he and his wife, Barbara, need the money to support two daughters (Joe's stepdaughters), and a lifestyle that includes a brick house in the nearby community of Christiansburg, two cars, occasional vacations, and a time-share at a ski resort. Barbara works fulltime at a factory that makes engine bearings, but she never works overtime, so that she can spend more time with her daughters. Joe Sizemore earned about $47,000—including overtime—in 1996, and his wife's paycheck gave them a combined income of $75,000. According to *The Wall Street Journal*'s Aeppel, Mrs. Sizemore supports Joe's decision to work long overtime hours, ``. . . though she often wishes he could spend more time with the family.''[14]

The Corning factory is often dusty and noisy, and much of the work is monotonous. One such job is standing at the production line for long hours examining parts for flaws, but a more interesting one for Joe is ``dry blending,'' which involves pouring raw materials into large hoppers that supply the machines that produce the ceramic cores. Working long hours has produced some conflicts and tradeoffs in Joe's life. He has had to give up hunting and fishing, as well as collecting Star Trek memorabilia. He often sees his wife only a few hours a day, and spends much of the free time that he does have working on his house. Both Joe and Barbara seem to be in good health, but after a vacation in Florida they decided they both needed to lose weight and have begun eating healthier, low-fat foods.

Joe deals with the stress of the long hours that he works at the plant by using humor, unlike some other workers who daydream or do mental puzzles.

> His specialty is impersonations and reciting skits from old episodes of ``Saturday Night Live.'' His coworkers like his clowning, even citing it on his most recent peer-review report as one of his strengths. Assessing himself, Mr. Sizemore says: ``I'm doing a lot better than I every thought I would do,'' noting, ``I don't have any special skill—I'm not a welder or a bricklayer. I didn't finish college.''[15]

He has thought about doing other things, such as owning his own landscape business, but he says that as long as the factory continues to employ him, he will keep working at the plant.

Questions for Discussion and Reflection

1. If values drive action, what do Joe Sizemore's actions tell us about his values?

2. Do Mr. Sizemore's long hours at the plant conflict with other aspects of his life? How would you describe his personal balancing act?

3. Are Mr. Sizemore's values and actions congruent with Corning's? Is he creating value for his employer?

4. Looking at Mr. Sizemore's lifestyle from a long-term perspective, do you think it is viable? Does the author of the article give us a hint that Mr. Sizemore is considering some other options?

5. From your personal perspective, how do you feel about the way Mr. Sizemore lives? Do you have the right to judge him?

Endnotes

1. Arno Penzias, "New Paths to Success," *Fortune*, 12 June 1995, 90–94.
2. Ibid.
3. Gareth S. Gardiner, *21st Century Manager* (Princeton, NJ: Peterson's/Pacesetter Books, 1996).
4. Ibid., 144–145.
5. Laura D'Andrea Tyson, "Why the Wage Gap Just Keeps Getting Bigger and Bigger," *Business Week*, 14 December 1998, 22.
6. Ibid.
7. Robert H. Waterman, Jr., Judith A. Waterman, and Betsy A. Collard, "Toward a Career-Resilient Workforce," *Harvard Business Review*, July-August 1994, 87–95.
8. Gardiner, *21st Century Manager*, 187–188.
9. William Bridges, "A Nation of Owners," *Inc.*, 16 May 1995, 89–91.
10. Ibid.
11. Nathaniel Branden, *The Psychology of Self-Esteem* (Los Angeles: Nash Publishing, 1969).
12. Nathaniel Branden, *Taking Responsibility* (New York: Simon & Schuster, 1996).
13. Timothy Aeppel, "Living Overtime: A Factory Workaholic," *The Wall Street Journal*, 13 October 1998, sec. B, p. 1.
14. Ibid., sec. B, p. 22.
15. Ibid.

Epilogue

We have returned again and again in the pages of this book—and purposefully—to two major themes of Value Driven Management: that organizational decision makers at every level (all employees) must make decisions that maximize value over time for the organization, and that individuals are responsible for maximizing their personal value over time. Individuals and organizations should strive to make the two compatible. Value Driven Management is not intended to replace other management theories, methods, tools, or schools of thought; instead it is a comprehensive and multidimensional philosophy of management that we believe establishes a conceptual foundation for other approaches to leading and managing.

Value Driven Management does not at all propose that shareholders/owners are not entitled to returns on their investments that are commensurate with the risks they have taken. It does not attempt to replace profitability—as we have noted repeatedly—as an appropriate function of a for-profit organization. The process of juggling and balancing eight value drivers that impact the organization, however, requires the very best business and managerial judgment, as well as the sustained commitment of the entire organization to maximizing value over time. It is clear that by properly taking into account what all its constituent groups value, the organization cannot fail to maximize value over time for itself.

Value Driven Management is simply not a zero-sum game. It is in fact a classic example of "win-win" management in action, where the organization and the individuals associated with it will maximize value over the long haul. It is also a philosophy that will help decision makers at every level develop the wisdom and judgment that will help them withstand the tremendous pressures virtually every organization faces in a globalized world where the pace of change continues to accelerate. We are reminded of the wise observation of the late Dr. W. Edwards Deming, who once remarked that it is simply wrong to assume that developing quality must run counter to lowering costs. He knew that Total Quality Management is not a zero-sum game, and neither is Value Driven Management. We encourage our readers to consider our philosophy of management, to engage in genuine dialogue with other decision makers about it, and to refine and implement it faithfully and conscientiously in their personal and organizational lives. We believe that good things will happen—and that value will be created—for organizations and all their constituents in a brave and bold new millennium.

Appendix A

Solution to the Four-Dots Puzzle

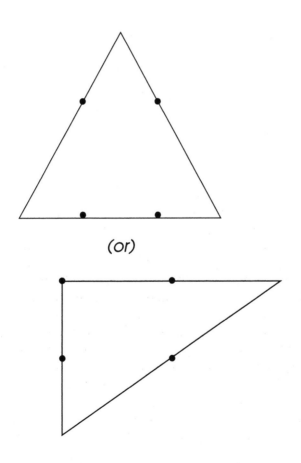

(or)

Appendix B

A Detailed Description of the Eighteen Value Dimensions Contained in the Organization Value Congruency and Satisfaction Scale (OVCSS)

1. *Autonomy*—This dimension has to do with whether the job/organization allows a great deal of autonomy or individual discretion with regard to how a job is completed, as long as the desired results are obtained.

2. *Creativity*—This dimension has to do with whether the job/organization allows for a great deal of individual creativity and expression, and encourages this in one's approach to the work.

3. *Complexity*—This dimension has to do with whether the job/organization requires a great deal of complexity, in thinking and action, in carrying out one's work. This entails dealing with a number of different interrelated and difficult concepts, with

effective results dependent upon managing the work process correctly.

4. *Intensity*—This dimension has to do with the physical and mental intensity of a work environment or a particular job. It may be that the work is very fast-paced or interrupted a great many times, or requires great concentration, or involves dealing with a lot of very difficult situations that greatly raise the level of stress and intensity.

5. *Status*—This dimension deals with the perceived importance of the job/organization within which the individual works.

6. *Precision*—This dimension describes a job or work environment where precision is extremely important. If mistakes are made, the impact could be significant on the desired outcomes.

7. *Competition*—This dimension has to do with the competitive nature of a particular job/organization. Some jobs require a great deal of competition in some form or another, either with internal or external people and factors, and other jobs do not.

8. *Physical Work*—This dimension simply describes the amount of physical work required in the position.

9. *Outdoor Work*—This dimension, naturally enough, deals with the amount of outdoor work involved or acquired in the job/organization.

10. *Security*—This dimension deals with how secure one's job/organization is on an ongoing basis.

11. *Routine*—This dimension has to do with how routine the nature of the work is, and if the ongoing work of the job/organization is somewhat repetitive and largely unchanging in the short term.

12. *People Oriented*—This dimension deals with the extent to which jobs/organizations are highly people oriented and require a great deal of interaction, compatibility, and strong interpersonal or "people" skills.

13. *Team Oriented*—This dimension describes the extent to which the job/organization requires a great deal of skill and time in working with others in self-directed or other types of teams.

14. *Travel*—This dimension deals with how much travel is required by a job/organization.

15. *Leadership/Authority*—This dimension describes the degree to which the position/organization requires a strong leadership ability and skills, and the degree to which individuals can exercise authority.

16. *Managing*—This dimension deals with whether the management of people and other resources on a day-to-day basis is a major portion of the position.

17. *Responsibility*—This dimension has to do with the level of responsibility one has for the outcomes of a particular job/organization.

18. *Industry Image*—This dimension deals with the image and prestige of the entire industry, not just the job/organization.

Index